To Dick and Michelle

SELECTED TITLES FROM THE BERKSHIRE TRAVELLER PRESS

Country Inns and Back Roads, North America
Country Inns and Back Roads, Europe
Farm, Ranch & Country Vacations
The Inn Way . . . Caribbean
Canada's Capital Inside Out
New Brunswick Inside Out

A Guide to
Music
Festivals
in
America

Carol Price Rabin

CLASSICAL, OPERA,
JAZZ, RAGTIME, AND DIXIELAND
POPS AND LIGHT CLASSICAL
FOLK AND TRADITIONAL
BLUEGRASS, OLD-TIME FIDDLERS,
AND COUNTRY

The Berkshire Traveller Press
STOCKBRIDGE, MASSACHUSETTS

FOREWORD

Twenty-five years ago, the serious concertgoer looked towards the summer season with a sense of approaching famine. In a few areas, a trying automobile trip could reward a diligent listener with a good concert, or a New Yorker could brave city heat, landing planes from La Guardia field, and a possible rain-out to hear a concert in the acoustical disaster of Lewisohn Stadium. With the few exceptions such as Chautauqua or Tanglewood, most of the country did without concerts for the summer months.

The intervening years have brought us to the point where (in spite of the fast food chains, fuel shortages, brown-outs, and other hot weather phenomena), the United States enjoys a profusion of fine summer music festivals that offer a most marvelous feast for the most demanding concertgoer.

The word festival implies a celebration and while some festivals are general in content, others seek to celebrate in a more specific manner: baroque music, opera, contemporary, Mostly Somebody, and whose one-hundredth birthday is it this year!?

Coast-to coast, May to September, indoor-outdoor, accessible-remote; the variety is almost endless! Use this guide; write early for programs, accommodations, tickets, and create your *own* summer festival.

JOSEPH SILVERSTEIN
Concertmaster
Boston Symphony Orchestra

Library; of Congress Card #78-73844
ISBN 0-912944-51-X
Copyright 1979 by Carol Price Rabin

"For the wise man, every day is a festival."
Plutarch

PREFACE

The words *music festival* conjure up in my mind a feeling, an atmosphere, rather than a specific place or setting — of a sharing with others, of pleasure, of excitement, relaxation, and fun. There is something about live music experienced in unusual and beautiful surroundings (often in the open air amidst the beauties of nature) that is truly transporting — electric, exciting — even joyous. The sensation of hearing and seeing an actual performance and "soaking up" the atmosphere has given me many unique and memorable musical experiences. And for many people such as myself, whose love of music is matched only by their enthusiasm for new, interesting, and beautiful places, the music festival is particularly ideal.

Perhaps that explains why I am an inveterate and enthusiastic festival-goer and adventuresome traveler, and also why I felt the need for a practical and selective guide to help me find music festivals which have been springing up in increasing numbers all over the country in the last few years. When I failed to find a readily-available source of such information, I decided to "do it myself." Naturally, one can never accomplish such an undertaking without a great deal of help. There were festivals I was unable to attend personally, and my grateful thanks are now offered to the staff members of all the festivals who answered my queries so promptly, giving me much valuable information, and who were so helpful in every way. I also wish to thank Paul Hwoschinsky and Dorothy Elia Howells for encouraging me to undertake the writing of the book, and Virginia Rowe for her invaluable help, advice, and guidance in editing all of the material.

A Guide to Musical Festivals in America is not only a musical travel-guide and a unique record of an important segment of the American musical world, but I believe all lovers of music will find it a means of broadening and enriching their musical experience.

Students, collectors, and librarians also will find this a helpful reference, and the Suggested Reading List an excellent additional source of material.

Although there has been no attempt to make this book all-inclusive, over 120 festivals in 39 states are represented, arranged under the categories of Classical, Opera, Jazz, Pops, Folk, Bluegrass, Old-Time Fiddlers, and Country. Rock festivals, being of a rather transitory nature, have not been included.

On a practical level, I urge my readers before traveling long distances to check specifically festival seasons and prices, inasmuch as they are often subject to change. The Ticket Information Section at the end of each description provides the necessary addresses and telephone numbers. During the festival seasons, both large and small communities are often booked well in advance or have only limited accommodations. I recommend that the reader write directly for accommodations either to the Visitor's Bureaus or the Chambers of Commerce indicated in the book.

I am continually searching out new festivals and would welcome any additional information on festivals to enrich and update future editions.

My hope for this book is that it will, in a world of electronics, tape, and plastic discs, open the door to another world of spontaneity and enjoyment —the world of music festivals.

CONTENTS

(For alphabetical listing of festivals by name, see Index.)

CLASSICAL

OPERA

JAZZ, RAGTIME, AND DIXIELAND

POPS AND LIGHT CLASSICAL

FOLK AND TRADITIONAL

BLUEGRASS, OLD-TIME FIDDLERS, AND COUNTRY

CLASSICAL

BIRMINGHAM FESTIVAL OF THE ARTS
Birmingham, Alabama
April for ten days

To many, Birmingham is a thoroughly American city, but it also has its cosmopolitan side, and has made many friends the world over for nearly thirty years with its Festival of the Arts. Each spring the festival pays tribute to a different nation, and the culture of the chosen country leaves a distinctive mark upon the festivities. Spain, France, Germany, Brazil, Greece, Austria, Belgium, and Canada are some of the countries most recently honored. The 1978 concerts highlighting Belgian music were particularly noteworthy as Flor Peeters, Belgium's leading organ composer, performed a wide repertoire ranging from Bach to César Franck (the Belgian-born French composer). He also played some of his own compositions. Many fine all-Flemish programs of sacred and secular music from the fifteenth and sixteenth centuries were also presented, along with a magnificent art exhibit of "Rubens and Humanism."

The Birmingham Symphony Orchestra is the participating ensemble, giving symphonic concerts and accompanying the opera, ballet, and the Civic Chorus. Some of the invited performers have been Anna Moffo, Florence Kopleff, June Anderson, André Watts, Frits Celis, and Christian Altenburger, as well as top-rank performers from each featured country. Since its beginning in 1951, when the Women's Committee of the Birmingham Symphony Orchestra started the festival, support has come from business groups, local citizens, colleges, and universities.

The calendar of events for each season covers the entire spectrum of performing arts: ballet, modern dance, art exhibits, light opera, films, musical performances of many varieties, lectures, seminars, and community events. Many facilities throughout the city are used for the festival programs: the Municipal Auditorium, Birmingham-Jefferson Civic Center with its 3,000-seat concert hall, Birmingham Southern College, various churches, theaters, and Woodrow Wilson Park.

For information write to: Birmingham Festival of the Arts Association, Suite 1004, Woodward Building, 1927 First Avenue North, Birmingham, Alabama 35203. Telephone: (205) 323-5461.

For accommodations write to: Greater Birmingham Convention and Visitors Bureau, 1909 Seventh Avenue North, Birmingham, Alabama 35203. Telephone: (205) 252-9825.

ALASKA FESTIVAL OF MUSIC
Anchorage, Alaska
Mid-June for ten days

One of the most memorable events in the history of the Alaska Festival of Music was a concert in 1970 when the programming spanned the so-called generation gap. The world-renowned contemporary composer, Dave Brubeck, appeared with his two sons: seventeen-year-old Christopher on the trombone and Daniel, fourteen, on drums. The songs were a combination of the new, old, and religious, and the audience went wild with enthusiasm. Brubeck also performed his own cantata, *The Light in the Wilderness,* and the "heads were nodding in rhythm, toes tapping, bodies swaying in the auditorium . . . people were involved." This concert was so successful that Brubeck returned in 1977 with three sons in the program: "Two Generations of Brubeck," a concert by America's first family of jazz.

The festival was started in 1956 by Mary Hale, one of Anchorage's most energetic patrons of the arts. She convinced Julius Herford and Robert Shaw to "come North" and direct the initial musical events. From this beginning, the festival has grown into a major cultural event. The festival lives up to its claim of "Music to Match our Mountains," and although it has run into a few obstacles, it has survived. The frontier spirit of its supporters has overcome both natural and manmade disasters, including the severe earthquake of 1964, and a strike which was halted by the Governor so that the "show could go on."

The programs include symphonic and chamber music, recitals, opera, and jazz, and each year a major choral work is performed by the Festival Chorus and Orchestra. The repertoire is varied and includes music from Bach's era to contemporary works. Guest conductors, musicians, ensembles, and dance groups are invited each year, many to return in subsequent years. Rainer Miedel, conductor and music director of the Seattle Symphony, has been engaged as guest conductor and music director at the

Alaska Festival for the 1977 and 1978 seasons. Some of the outstanding talent in recent years has been Richard Woltach, Michael Charry, Richard Kapp, Gunther Schuller, and Robert Shaw, conductors; Ani Kavafian, Oscar Peterson, Pepe Romero, Walter Trampler, instrumentalists; Dennis Bailey, Simon Estes, Archie Drake, Douglas Lawrence, and Gloria Marinacci, vocalists. Past seasons have featured such groups as the Sitka Festival Ensemble, Nikolais Dance Theatre, Eglevsky Ballet, New England Conservatory Ragtime, and Anchorage Woodwind Quintet.

The concerts are held in the evenings at several locations: the 1,000-seat Anchorage Performing Arts Center, West High School with seating for 2,500, and at a local church or theater.

An extension of the festival was initiated in 1963 when a number of young native Alaskans were chosen to attend the concerts and carry back to their villages or towns "the festival story." Another unique feature is King's Lake Fine Arts Camp where young Alaskan students study with local and guest musicians during the summer.

For tickets and information write to: Alaska Festival of Music, Post Office Box 325, Anchorage, Alaska 99510. Telephone: (907) 272-3022.

For accommodations write to: Anchorage Chamber of Commerce, 612 F Street, Anchorage, Alaska 99510. Telephone: (907) 272-2401.

SITKA SUMMER MUSIC FESTIVAL
Sitka, Alaska
First week in June
for three consecutive Tuesdays and Fridays

Sitka, Alaska, occasionally referred to as "The Paris of the Pacific," has exquisite coastal and mountain scenery, a fine Eskimo culture, the oldest Russian Orthodox Church in North America, a National Historic Park, a colorful heritage and past, and its own musical festival! The Sitka Festival was founded by Paul Rosenthal, violin virtuoso, who with the assistance of four other musicians produced the first musical event in 1972. The programs feature chamber music in various combinations, and the repertoire emphasizes the great classics of the eighteenth and nineteenth centuries. Before the festival came to town, the Sitkans were not particularly noted as chamber music devotees, but reports are that five string quartets performed in one season recently, and "nobody was complaining about the supposedly austere combinations of instruments. They loved it. It speaks well for the educational process that has been going on in Sitka since 1972."

A concert to be remembered above all others was in 1974 when the guest artist, Gregor Piatigorsky, world-renowned cellist, gave a concert with the festival regulars. The audience was ecstatic about the performance and the artist, and in turn Piatigorsky exhibited his enthusiasm for the warmth and the beauty of the community.

The festival's music director, Paul Rosenthal, performs each season with the festival's "regulars": Christiaan Bor, Yukiko Kamei, Paul Rosenthal, violin; Milton Thomas, viola; Jeffrey Solow, Godfried Hoogeveen, and Nathaniel Rosen, cello; Edward Auer, Jerome Lowenthal, and Doris Stevenson, piano. Other guest artists who have made their appearance have been Mitchell Lurie, Ani Kavafian, Gregor Piatigorsky, Berl Senofsky, and Walter Trampler.

Concerts are held in the elegant, contemporary, 500-seat Centennial Building auditorium which provides a beautiful and dramatic setting for the audience. There is a wall of glass behind the stage, and as it remains light throughout the concerts, patrons look out to the Sitka Sound and the high mountains of Baranof Island, to boats gliding past, and even to an occasional eagle or raven swooping by.

A visit to the festival in the historic community of Sitka promises superlative richness to the ears, as well as to the eyes!

For information write to: Sitka Summer Music Festival, Post Office Box 907, Sitka, Alaska 99835. Telephone: (907) 747-6076.

For accommodations write to: Sitka Chamber of Commerce, Post Office Box 638, Sitka, Alaska 99835. Telephone: (907) 747-8604.

FLAGSTAFF SUMMER FESTIVAL
Flagstaff, Arizona
*First week in June to the first week in August
for eight weeks*

Shoot-outs at Cracker Barrel Store, White Mountain Apache All-Indian Powwows, the Annual World Championship Inner Tube Race, and the Flagstaff Summer Festival are a few of the many interesting special events offered in Arizona throughout the year. Flagstaff, during the festival months, has a delightful summer climate and its American Indian culture and scenic

surroundings make it an ideal location to begin sightseeing excursions in any direction. The famed Grand Canyon National Park, only seventy-nine miles north of Flagstaff, is one of the world's outstanding natural wonders.

The Flagstaff Summer Festival is the major annual performing and visual arts festival in Arizona. Started as a music camp in the early 1960s under the sponsorship of Northern Arizona University, it soon became so successful that the Arizona Commission on Arts and Humanities encouraged its development into a full-fledged festival in 1966. The first year, Izler Solomon was conductor with the Indianapolis Symphony and the festival ran one week with eight musical events. Since then it has been extended into an eight-week festival with over twelve symphonic and chamber music concerts, ballet, theater, film presentations, Indian arts and crafts, art exhibits, and children's programs. Some of the artists who have appeared over the years are John Browning, Donald Gramm, Byron Janis, Grant Johannesen, Los Angeles Ballet Company, Leonard Pennario, Roberta Peters, Preservation Hall Jazz Band, Zara Nelsova, Alicia Schachter, and Laslo Varga. The concerts are held on the campus of Northern Arizona University in the Ardrey Music Hall with seating for 1,503 patrons.

From 1966 to 1977 Izler Solomon directed and conducted the

festival orchestra which was composed of musicans from Phoenix, Tucson, and Flagstaff symphonies. In 1978, Maurice Peress became music director and was one of the first people to be involved in a music education project for the United States Bureau of Indian Affairs. Maestro Peress toured Indian reservations in the Southwest in order to introduce music programs to Indian children. He likes to tell a story of a concert he conducted in Carthage, Missouri, when he saw three Indians sitting in the audience in the front row of the concert who had travelled over a hundred miles to hear the first performance of a work by an Indian composer, Louis Ballard!

For ticket information write to: Flagstaff Summer Festival Post Office Box 1607, Flagstaff, Arizona 86002. Telephone: (602) 774-5055.

For accommodations write to: Chamber of Commerce of Flagstaff, 101 W. Santa Fe Avenue, Flagstaff, Arizona 86001. Telephone: (602) 774-4505.

BACH FESTIVAL
Carmel, California
Mid-July for two weeks

Considered the quiet and unpretentious "Seacoast of Bohemia" in the early 1900s, Carmel, California has grown into a chic, busy, and bustling resort and artist community. Famous for its scenic beauty—white sandy beaches, a dramatic seventeen-mile drive—and its quaint streets lined with art galleries and craft shops, "the Village" is also well-known for its annual Bach Festival. The event started in 1935 when an assemblage of localites—a dentist, a carpenter, a photographer, a socialite, and a butcher, pursued their vocations by day and their avocation, music-making, by night. They performed in an art gallery owned by Miss Dene Denny and Miss Hazel Watrous, both of whom were keenly interested in music and art, and encouraged the amateur musicians to open their weekly rehearsals to subscribers. The art gallery soon overflowed with patrons, and from these gatherings the Penha Piano Quartet evolved, and later developed into the fifty-piece Monterey Peninsula Orchestra. With a fifty-voice chorale under the direction of Miss Denny, both musical groups—the orchestra and the chorale—evolved into what today is known as the Bach Festival.

Although the festival emphasizes the works of J.S. Bach, the works of other seventeenth and eighteenth-century composers —Mozart, Vivaldi, Haydn, Telemann, and Handel are also played. The programs include major choral works, cantatas, chamber music, and solo recitals. Sandor Salgo, music director since 1956, conducts the Festival Orchestra; Priscilla Salgo, the Festival Chorale; and Kenneth Ahrens, the Festival Chorus.

Recent guest performers include Raymond Gibbs, Klara Barlow, Douglas Lawrence, David Abel, Carol Vaness, Jess Thomas, Thomas Paul, Walter Trampler, Pamela South, and Malcolm Hamilton. Of a 1977 concert version of Beethoven's *Fidelio* with singers Barlow, Lawrence, Paul, and Thomas, it was reported, "You will not hear a better *Fidelio* from anyone, anywhere . . . not even in Salzburg!"

Concerts are held daily during the festival with a recital in the morning, followed by another recital midday and an evening concert. Most of the concerts are held in the steep-gabled stucco Sunset Center Theatre with seating for 730 patrons. Other concerts are held in the historic Carmel Mission Basilica seating 430 patrons.

This mission built in 1771 by Father Junipero Serra has an adjoining courtyard and garden with native plants, and is considered one of the most charming and attractive of all of Father Serra's twenty-one missions. Other concerts, lectures, and recitals take place in the Parish Hall, All Saints' Episcopal Church, and at various other locations throughout the village.

For tickets write to: Carmel Bach Festival, P.O. Box 575, Carmel, California 93921. Telephone: (408) 624-1521.

For accommodations write to: Carmel Business Association, Box 4444, Carmel, California 93921. Telephone: (408) 624-2522.

CABRILLO MUSIC FESTIVAL
Aptos, California
Mid-August for ten days

A "moveable festival" is what the Cabrillo Music Festival calls itself, but it does have a home base—Cabrillo College Theatre in Aptos, California. The "moveable" refers to the many unique and picturesque sites where concerts are performed—Mission

San Juan Baustista, the First United Methodist Church in Watsonville, Saint Joseph's Church in Capitola, Duck Island in San Lorenzo Park, and Coconut Grove in Santa Cruz. The festival started in 1963 when composers Louis Harrison and Robert Hughes worked with a handful of local residents to present small concerts in the lovely, secluded beach community of Aptos on Monterey Bay. Gerhard Samuel, then conductor of the Oakland Symphony, became music director and under his talented leadership the festival was an immediate success. Four years later Carlos Chavez, world-renowned composer, became director until he retired in 1974. Dennis Russell Davies, young and gifted conductor from the Saint Paul Chamber Orchestra, became music director at that time and has continued the tradition of innovative programs which respond to the community's diverse cultural and ethnic heritage and interests.

The festival orchestra presents orchestral and chamber works, concertos, staged operas, and solo recitals by professional musicians from the San Francisco and Los Angeles area. Music presented ranges from the baroque period to contemporary compositions—often those not usually performed during the regular concert season. Emphasis is also placed on presenting West Coast and world premieres with the composer of the particular work invited to be in attendance. Some of the composers-in-residence have been Charles Amirkhanian, Louis Ballard, William Bolcom, John Cage, Aaron Copland, Anthony Gnazzo, Robert Hughes, Lou Harrison, Keith Jarrett, Garrett List, Anthony Newman, Gerhard Samuel, and Francis Thorne. Guest artists in recent years have included Janis Hardy, William Masselos, Janos Starker, Paula Seibel, Joan Morris, Romuald Tecco, John Nelson, Kenneth Harrison, James Tocco, and William McGlaughlin.

The festival's location on picturesque Monterey Bay in northern California places a visitor in an excellent starting position to see the many beautiful sights of the area—Big Sur, Carmel-by-the-Sea, Santa Cruz, historic Monterey, the scenic seventeen-mile drive, Pebble Beach, and time permitting, Hearst Castle at San Simeon.

For ticket information write to: Cabrillo Music Festival, 6500 Soquel Drive, Aptos, California 95003. Telephone: (408) 688-6466.

For accommodations write to: Santa Cruz Area Chamber of Commerce, Church and Center Streets, Santa Cruz, California 95060. Telephone: (408) 423-1111.

HOLLYWOOD BOWL SUMMER SERIES
Hollywood, California
First week in July to the third week in September for eleven weeks

In the summer, "The Bowl" to a Westerner means only one thing: the Hollywood Bowl, and that in turn means a spectacle, glamour, fun and great music! Daisy Dell, as the area was called when the concerts began in 1922, was much like the setting for a western movie . . . nothing but sagebrush and chaparral! Musical productions continued though plagued by financial troubles, eviction notices, and the depression. In 1951, a heroic "Save the Bowl" campaign led by the energetic crusader for musical causes, Mrs. Norman Chandler, put the Hollywood Bowl back into a healthy financial condition where it has remained ever since.

The Bowl is the summer home of the Los Angeles Philharmonic with Ernest Fleischmann as general director since 1969; Zubin Mehta was music director from 1970 to 1978, and the 1979 season will see Carlo Maria Giulini as the new music director. Concerts are given at least three nights a week during the ten-week season, and patrons are offered a wide range from classical to pops and jazz. Also included are "spectaculars"—perhaps Tchaikovsky's 1812 Overture complete with cannon, military band, and fireworks; Children's Early Evening Concerts; and Marathon Concerts—six hours of uninterrupted music of a specific composer with attendance on a "come-as-you-like basis." The roster of guest conductors and artists is impressive, being drawn from the top ranks of the international performing circuit: conductors Sir John Barbirolli, Leonard Bernstein, Herbert von Karajan, Otto Klemperer, Josef Krips, Eugene Ormandy, Leonard Slatkin, Sir Georg Solti, Igor Stravinsky, George Szell, and Bruno Walter; artists like The Beatles, Jascha Heifetz, Bob Hope, Ethel Merman, Brigit Nilsson, Jessye Norman, David Oistrakh, Mstislav Rostropovich, Beverly Sills, Frank Sinatra, Isaac Stern, and Joan Sutherland. The Bowl has also served as a proving ground where many distinguished artists made their professional debuts on stage: Lucine Amara, Mariyln Horne, Mario Lanza, George London, Jerome Hines, and Lorin Maazel, the present director of the Cleveland Orchestra, who conducted the Los Angeles Philharmonic at the Bowl when he was ten!

At the place where the Hollywood Freeway cuts through the hills is a lovely 117-acre park covered with trees and shrubs. The natural amphitheater of the Hollywood Bowl, one of the largest in the world, is built up against the hillside, and sagebrush and chaparral are the natural backdrop. A huge acoustical shell, along with the natural acoustics of the hillside make perfect listening conditions for 17,000 patrons . . . an unaided voice can be heard in the back row! "Music Under the Stars" is indeed a valid claim, as most of the evenings are balmy and there have been only three or four evenings postponed because of rain in over fifty years!

For tickets and information write to: Hollywood Bowl Summer Festival c/o Los Angeles Philharmonic Association, 135 North Grand Avenue, Los Angeles, California 90012. Telephone: (213) 972-7300, and during the season: (213) 876-8742.

For accommodations write to: Los Angeles Convention and Visitors Bureau, 505 S. Flower Street, Los Angeles, California 90071. Telephone: (213) 488-9100.

IDYLLWILD MUSIC FESTIVAL
Idyllwild, California
Last weeks of August for two weeks

"Music in the mountains" (as distinguished from mountain music) is the theme of the Idyllwild School of Music and Art, better known as ISOMATA. Located forty miles southwest of Palm Springs and one hundred miles east of Los Angeles, the two-hundred-acre campus is an area of natural beauty, more than a mile above sea level and within the San Jacinto Mountain Range which has several peaks of over 10,000 feet. ISOMATA was established in 1950 by Dr. and Mrs. Max Krone, and the music festival was started in 1956 by the devoted work of the Krones, Robert Evans Holmes, and Ralph Rush. The campus site was donated in 1964 by the Idyllwild Arts Foundation to the University of Southern California and is maintained as a separate campus.

The school, under executive director Allen E. Koenig, offers study and instruction in drama, art, dance, writing, and music and strives "to produce an environment where aspiring artists can come together with master artists in a residential setting and engage in serious learning." The mountain campus operates ten or eleven weeks, and the music festival, which is given the last two weeks of the session, represents the culmination of intensive study by the choir, wind ensemble, and the orchestra. The festival concerts include eight or nine programs of orchestra, choral, and chamber music with repertoire ranging from J.S. Bach to Henry Cowell. Robert G. Hasty and Robert Evans Holmes, emeritus director, conduct the 125 vocalists in the Festival Choir; Larry G. Curtis conducts the ninety-five piece Festival Wind Ensemble; and John Koshak, conducts the eighty-piece Festival Symphony Orchestra. All concerts are free and are held in the 300-seat Idyllwild Arts Foundation Theatre, except the final concert which is performed in the bowl, accommodating 1,000 people. The final concert in 1978 ended on a high note — the Wind Ensemble faculty gave a premiere performance of Philip Westin's *Ballet for Bubbles (An Ode for a Liberated Hippo)!*

For information write to: Idyllwild School of Music and the Arts (ISOMATA), Idyllwild Campus, Univeristy of Southern California, Post Office Box 38, Idyllwild, California 92349. Telephone: (714) 659-2171.

For accommodations write to: Chamber of Commerce, 54200 No. Circle, Idyllwild, California 92349. Telephone: (714) 659-3259.

MUSIC AT THE VINEYARDS
Saratoga, California
July and August for three weekends

Wine and music, a natural cultural blend, come together at Music at the Vineyards held at the Paul Masson Mountain Winery, one hour south of San Francisco in Saratoga, California. The concert series was initiated in 1958 by Norman Fromm, a member of a music-loving family which was one of the owners of the winery. Fromm felt that the setting was unique and would be conducive to an excellent concert series and wanted to share his love of fine music and the beauty of the area with the community.

The series includes music that is infrequently performed — unusual classical music of the great masters. Programming ranges from baroque to modern, and since 1970 emphasis has been placed on presenting new works commissioned by the series. Outstanding composers, generally Californians, have had their works performed and include Grant Beglarian, Richard

Felciano, Andrew Imbrie, Wayne Peterson, David del Tredici, and Heuwell Tircuit. Sandor Salgo, music director since 1964, often conducts the ensembles at the series. Although emphasis is not placed on so-called box office attractions, Music at the Vineyards has invited outstanding performers recognized for their skilled interpretations of the music performed. Guest conductors, soloists, and ensembles who have recently been heard at the concerts include artists Stuart Canin, Arthur Fiedler, Jaime Laredo, Bonnie Hampton, Marta Le Roux, David Glazer, Eudice Shapiro, Calvin Simmons, and Zvi Zeitlin; and ensembles: Alma Trio, American Brass Quintet, Beaux Arts String Quartet, Lenox Quartet, Opera Comique of San Francisco, the New York Woodwind Quintet, and San Francisco Vineyard Ensemble.

The winery is located atop a mountain in the Santa Cruz Mountain Range where concertgoers are treated to a 360-degree view of the mountains and the Santa Clara Valley below. The original winery, set amid vineyards that yield varietal grapes, was built in 1858 and provides a backdrop for a natural amphitheater where the concerts are held. There is no artificial amplification, and yet 1000 patrons regularly attest to near-perfect acoustics. Concerts are given on Saturday and Sunday afternoons, and as the days are usually warm and sunny, concerts are scheduled to start in the late afternoon. On the weekends when the Music at the Vineyard Series is not in session, either the Merola Opera Program presents a fine baroque opera in English, or Vintage Sounds, a jazz series, occupies the amphitheater.

Music at the Vineyards is noted both for its tastefully chosen repertoire and adept musicians, and for its gracious and relaxed atmosphere. Patrons are surrounded not only by the delicious fragrance of the vineyards during the concerts, but at intermission, champagne is served courtesy of Paul Masson Vineyards! It was Ralph Waldo Emerson who said, "Music and wine are one." This certainly holds true for Music at the Vineyards, since the concert series keeps improving with age, just like a good Cabernet.

For information and tickets write to: Music at the Vineyards, P.O. Box 97, Saratoga, California 95070. Telephone: (408) 257-7800.

For accommodations write to: Saratoga Chamber of Commerce, Post Office Box 161, Saratoga, California 95070. Telephone: (408) 867-0753.

MUSIC FROM BEAR VALLEY
Bear Valley, California
Last week in July to the second week in August for three weekends

Abandoned mining camps, gold rush ghost towns, and beautiful alpine scenery are all a part of a visit to Bear Valley and its music festival. In the lofty mountains of Alpine County in northern California is a tall pine wilderness area surrounded by national and state parks which can truly lay claim to producing music in a rarified (7,200 feet high) atmosphere!

Envisioned as a "musician's workshop and retreat" by its founder, John Gosling, in 1969, the festival includes traditional, as well as contemporary music. Maestro Gosling, who also holds the title of artistic director and conductor of the Northern Carolina Symphony Orchestra, has introduced open rehearsals in Bear Valley whereby patrons are exposed to practice sessions which exhibit the interplay of ideas and music between artists. Musicians are also encouraged to plan the repertoire for their own programs and to perform impromptu concerts. The festival orchestra is composed of professional musicians chosen from orchestras throughout the United States and Canada, and comprises the basic ensemble for orchestral and chamber music, accompaniment of soloists and instrumentalists, and for the opera productions. Guest artists invited to the festival in recent years have been pianists John Browning, Lili Kraus, and Eugene List; violinists Carroll Glen and Stuart Canin; vocalists Joan Barber, William Brown, Hilda Harris, Gwendolyn Jones, Carol Nielsen, and William Wahman; and cellist Geoffrey Rutkowski. Bear Valley Lodge was the site of the festival concerts until 1976, when all of the "sounds of music" moved to a specially designed red and white tent seating 750 concertgoers.

If one lingers awhile at Bear Valley there are a wide variety of activities in the summer—tennis, hiking, swimming, fishing, riding, sailing, and of course, the music festival. And nearby is the Mother Lode country where gold was discovered in the 1850s. Such towns as Sutter Creek, Dogtown, Jackson, Mokelumne Hill, Murphys, and Angels Camp (where the famous Frog Jumping Contest is held each year) are all a part of California's exciting past and provide fascinating sightseeing excursions!

For tickets and information write to: Music from Bear Valley P.O. Box 68, Bear Valley, California 95223. Telephone: (209) 753-2311.

For accommodations write to: Bear Valley Central Reservations, Box

8, Bear Valley, California 95223. Telephone: (209) 753-2311 or
Calaveras County Chamber of Commerce, Altaville, California
95221. Telephone: (209) 736-0170.

OJAI FESTIVAL
Ojai, California
Late May for three days

The Ojai Festival may not have the amenities of some of the
larger summer festivals, but it holds its own and then some with
its fine musical presentations. In 1926, music devotee Mrs.
Sprague Coolidge sponsored chamber music concerts in Ojai,
but it was not until twenty years later that the devoted work of
Mr. and Mrs. John Bauer and colleagues officially launched the
Ojai Festival. In 1947, it opened grandly with a recital by the
world-renowned French baritone, Martial Singher.

The Ojai Festival's strength lies in its strong interest and
support of modern music. While the always-interesting programs range from early baroque to the avant-garde, and emphasis is placed on discovery or rediscovery of rare works of the
great masters, Ojai has gained its international reputation by
presenting the "music of today." Premieres are an important
focus with composers, if available, invited to conduct their own
compositions. Some of the composers whose works have been
premiered in recent years are, Lukas Foss, William Kraft,
Frederick Lesemann, Karlheinz Stockhausen, David del Tredici,
and Charles Wuorinen.

The Ojai Festival Chamber Orchestra composed of professional musicans from the Santa Barbara and Los Angeles area
performs during the season, as well as invited ensembles such as
the Boston Symphony Chamber Players, the Juilliard, La Salle,
and the Paganini Quartets, the Los Angeles Philharmonic
Orchestra, and the Roger Wagner Chorale. A brief sampling of
the guest artists includes conductors Pierre Boulez, Aaron
Copland, Calvin Simmons, Igor Stravinsky, and Michael Tilson
Thomas; and performers Edward Auer, Marvellee Cariaga,
Marilyn Horne, Lili Kraus, Jonathan Mack, Gregor Piatigorsky,
André Previn, and Eudice Shapiro.

The festival is located in Ojai, a small community fifteen miles
inland from the Pacific Ocean near Ventura in southern
California. It is a quiet and beautiful town nestled in a valley in
the steep verdant Topatopa Mountain range. Concerts are held
in the center of town in Libbey Park. A huge, arched, old

sycamore tree provides shade for the bowl and was the inspiration for the asymetrical facade of the orchestra shell. Wooden benches provide seating for 1,000 listeners and the expansive lawn provides additional seating for many other concertgoers. The atmosphere is relaxed, cordial, and informal; the facilities, rustic. There are no dressing rooms and some patrons recall seeing Igor Stravinsky sitting on a camp stool outside a makeshift tent assembled for him during the festival. And another year during a concert, a huge blackbird kept flying up on the stage during a flute solo. It finally flew away when it realized it had not found a feathered friend.

Ojai Festival's smallness and uniqueness can be deceiving, for it is a highly sophisticated, prestigious music festival popular with those in the know!

For information write to: Ojai Music Festival, Post Office Box 185, Ojai, California 93023. Telephone: (805) 646-2094.

For accommodations write to: Ojai Chamber of Commerce, 111 West Santa Ana Street, Ojai, California 93022. Telephone: (805) 646-3000.

SAN FRANCISCO SYMPHONY SUMMER SERIES
Concord, California
Last three weeks in August for three weekends

"The Symphony Goes Casual at Concord" has been the password of the San Francisco Symphony Summer Concert series. The musical and social emphasis is on relaxed enjoyment, for audiences can listen to great music under the stars in a rural setting ideal for picnicking and fun with family and friends. For many years the San Francisco Symphony had presented Pops Concerts with Arthur Fiedler in the Civic Auditorium in downtown San Francisco, as well as giving a few concerts in a Concord city park in conjunction with the Concord Jazz Festival. When the new Concord pavilion was opened in 1975, the San Francisco Symphony Orchestra gave five concerts, thereby inaugurating a yearly series which has continued ever since.

Although the season is short compared to many major summer musical events throughout the country, the musical offerings at Concord are diverse and interesting with both classical and pops. A concert of special interest was in 1975 when Seiji Ozawa, then music director, introduced a novel work in three pieces by three renowned Japanese composers entitled,

Three Space (Ten, Chi, Jin) for the Orchestra which was inspired by Dag Hammarskjold's *Markings*. The musical work employed full orchestra along with Japanese instruments—biwa, non-kan, utai, shakuhachi, and drums.

Edo de Waart, music director since 1976, has shared the podium with such well-known conductors as James Conlon, Arthur Fiedler, André Kostelanetz, William Steinberg, Klaus Tennstedt, Michael Tilson Thomas, and David Zinman. Classical and popular music lovers have heard top rank artists such as Pearl Bailey, Louis Bellson, Montserrat Caballé, Misha Dichter, Christoph Eschenbach, Ella Fitzgerald, Benny Goodman, Lorin Hollander, Marilyn Horne, Peggy Lee, Jean-Pierre Rampal, Sarah Vaughan, and André Watts.

The concerts are given in Concord in the Mount Diablo foothills, thirty miles east of San Francisco. The pavilion at Concord, cited as one of the best acoustically engineered facilities in the country, provides fine listening for 3,555 concertgoers seated under the cover of the acre-square roof open on all three sides, as well as for the additional 5,000 who can be accommodated on the surrounding grassy lawn.

Hearing the San Francisco Symphony at Concord combines three irresistible elements indigenous to California—culture, pleasant climate, and casualness!

For information write to: Concord Series, San Francisco Symphony, 107 War Memorial Veterans Building, San Francisco, California 94102. Telephone; (415) 431-5400.

For accommodations write to: San Francisco Convention and Visitors Bureau, 1390 Market Street, San Francisco, California 94102. Telephone: (415) 626-5500.

SAN LUIS OBISPO MOZART FESTIVAL
San Luis Obispo, California
First week in August for six days

Will success spoil the San Luis Obispo Mozart Festival? It appears not at all, for each season it has expanded its programming and introduced new concepts—and each year is better than the last.

The notion of a festival originated with John Ellis, who was performing as a guest oboe soloist with the County Symphony in San Luis Obispo in 1970. Ellis suggested to three members of the Music Department faculty at California Polytechnic State University—John Russell, Ronald Ratcliffe, and Clifton Swanson that the setting and cultural climate was ideal for a music festival. No sooner said than done, for one year later the festival was inaugurated with Clifton Swanson as music director.

The event was conceived as a tribute to Wolfgang Amadeus Mozart, but it was decided that composers from all periods should be represented in order to create varied and interesting concerts. The programs include choral, orchestral, and chamber music recitals, and opera. The Festival Orchestra is composed of professional musicians from the West Coast with Clifton Swanson conducting the orchestra and John Russell leading the festival singers. Many regulars appear each year as guest artists—Louise Di Tullio, John Ellis, Donald Pippin, Peppe Romero, Michael Sells, Milton Thomas, Dorothy Wade, and James Weaver.

Some of the new concepts added to the festival's format in recent years have been Donald Pippin's Pocket Opera, Richard Bay's Puppet Opera, an Early Keyboard Instrument Symposium, and free instrumental clinics offered by the Mozart Festival and Cuesta College to music students from elementary school through college.

The majority of the concerts are held on the campus of California Polytechnic State University in the 500-seat Cal Poly Theatre, and to add a unique flavor the the festival, several concerts are scheduled elsewhere—the historic Mission San Luis Obispo de Tolsa, seating 550, established by Father Junipero Serra in 1772, and at the Veterans Memorial Building in Cambria, a small picturesque resort town north of San Luis Obispo.

The Mozart Festival is literally in the center of activity, as it is midway between San Francisco and Los Angeles. From that location one can travel north or south to attend many other music festivals up and down the Golden State.

For information write to: San Luis Obispo Mozart Festival Association, Post Office Box 311, San Luis Obispo, California 93406. Telephone: (805) 543-4580.

For accommodations write to: San Luis Obispo Chamber of Commerce, 1039 Chorro Street, San Luis Obispo, California 93401. Telephone: (805) 543-1323.

ASPEN MUSIC FESTIVAL
Aspen, Colorado
*Last week in June to the last week in August
for nine weeks*

Bastille Day, July 14, 1962, was a memorable day at the Aspen Music Festival, for not only were there activities commemorating French independence, but it was the celebration of Darius Milhaud's seventieth birthday. Milhaud, the world-famous composer, who had been a part of the festival since its beginning, was a familar sight at Aspen every summer, and was deeply loved and respected. Speeches were given, telegrams read from the Mayor of Aix-en-Provence, Milhaud's birthplace, and he was presented with the keys to the city of Aspen. Milhaud, visibly touched, said it was the first time anybody had given him the keys to any city! The final tribute was in the form of music. Milhaud took the podium and conducted his own compositions and the American premiere of his work, a harp concerto, *Chants Populaires Hebraiques.* The vocalist, a lady with an inconquerable spirit and a dearly beloved teacher at Aspen, was Jennie Tourel.

Aspen during the 1880s was one of Colorado's wealthiest communities, for with the discovery of silver, the ore rolled out of her mines at $15,000 a ton. Aspen lost its golden luster when silver ceased to be the standard currency and the legendary silver mining community soon became insignificant. Aspen's birth as a center of culture began in 1945, when Chicago industrialist Walter Paepcke decided that Aspen would be a suitable site for a Platonic community. An outgrowth of the Goethe Bicentennial Celebration in 1949 was the formation of the Aspen Music Festival and the Aspen Institute of Humanistic Studies.

The Aspen Music Festival, one of the most important musical events in the nation, rivals in terms of performances and training the prestigious Berkshire Music Festival at Tanglewood in Massachusetts. The Aspen School of Music operates in conjunction with the festival and claims a group of talented faculty-artists of 180 who are in residence during the summer. The school enrolls over 800 students for the nine-week period and offers seminars, master classes, open rehearsals, private instruction, and many performance opportunities. The roster of faculty-artists and guests reads like *Who's Who* and a few of the many distinguished artists include Adele Addison, Claus Adam, Misha Dichter, Maureen Forrester, Lawrence Foster, Lillian Fuchs, Lilian Kallir, Zara Nelsova, Thomas Paul, Walter Trampler, and Laszlo Varga, and such ensembles as the American Brass Quintet, American String Quartet, and the Cleveland Quartet. There are a number of ensembles performing weekly concerts — the Aspen Chamber Symphony, The Aspen Festival Orchestra, Chamber Music Concerts, and the Philharmonia. The students and the experienced professional musicians perform with all of the orchestras except for the Philharmonia, which is composed entirely of music school students.

The Conference on Contemporary Music, founded in 1958 by Darius Milhaud, is a very important part of the festival and is directed by Richard Dufallo. The Conference is scheduled for six days in August, and each season, a well-known musician is invited to be the "composer in residence," to introduce his compositions, and participate in seminars and lectures. Composers at previous conferences have included Luciano Berio, William Bolcom, Elliott Carter, Aaron Copland, Peter Maxwell Davies, Jacob Druckman, Oliver Knussen, Oliver Messiaen, Krzysztof Penderecki, Sir Michael Tippett, Virgil Thomson, Richard Wernick, and Charles Wuorinen. Another special group is the Choral Institue with director Fiora Contino. Both the Conference and the Institute offer concerts during the season.

Jorge Mester, music director of the Aspen Music Festival since 1970, has shared the podium with such well-known conductors as Sergiu Comissiona, Richard Dufallo, Sixten Ehrling, Erich Leinsdorf, Itzhak Perlman, Julius Rudel, and Leonard Slatkin.

The programming is varied and ranges from baroque to modern works. Maestro Mester claims that "as our audience is a very special, openminded group, we can program freely at the festival. We can give them Bach's Mass in B Minor one day, and Berezowsky's Suite for Seven Brass Instruments the next."

Aspen is a mood, an attitude, and one of the most beautiful alpine communities in the country. Nestled in a broad valley of the Roaring Fork River in the Rocky Mountain Range, Aspen, at an altitude of 7,900 feet is surrounded by seven peaks all towering over 14,000 feet. During the summer, the days are warm and sunny, except for an occasional thunderstorm which usually occurs just before the 4 P.M. concerts. The main concerts featuring symphonic orchestra or chamber music are staged four times a week in the large circular, white-tented amphitheater seating 1,600. Smaller ensembles, recitals, and seminars are held in the Paepcke Auditorium and the community church. Besides the concerts mentioned here, there are dozens of small musical offerings and master classes dotting the summer schedule and making it possible for the music enthusiast to indulge himself with the beautiful sounds of music every day of the season!

For tickets and information write to: Aspen Music Festival, Post Office Box AA, Aspen, Colorado 81611. Telephone: (303) 925-3254.

For accommodations write to: Aspen Chamber of Commerce, 328 East Hyman, Aspen, Colorado 81611. Telephone: (303) 925-1940.

MUSIC MOUNTAIN
Falls Village, Connecticut
Early July to early September
(ten Saturday and two Sunday afternoons)

New Yorkers may be proud of Caramoor and Bay Staters of Tanglewood, but Yankees from Connecticut feel blessed with Music Mountain, which claims to be the oldest continuing chamber music ensemble in North America. In northwestern Connecticut near Falls Village in the foothills of the Berkshires, and atop a 117-acre mountain resides the site of these fine musical events—Music Mountain. Jacques Gordon, concertmaster of the Chicago Symphony Orchestra, internationally renowned violinist, and founder of the Gordon Quartet, is credited with starting Music Mountain in 1929. With the help of many generous supporters, he built the concert hall and four homes to accommodate the members of the quartet. The 300-seat Gordon Hall is considered an "acoustical gem," for the design simulates the inside of a violin with solid wood everywhere except for the glass panes on the doors. Upon the death of Mr. Gordon in 1948, the quartet was renamed The Berkshire Quartet, with Music Mountain as its permanent home. Members of the quartet are cellist Fritz Magg; violinists Urico Rossi and Gino Sambuco (Magg and Rossi are both veterans having joined the quartet in 1940 and 1946 respectively); and violist Abraham Skernick.

Contemporary and classical works are presented, as well as some premiere works such as compositions of Bernard Heiden and Charles Shackford performed in 1977. Guest artist are invited each season so that works other than string quartets may be played. Recent years have included pianists Abba Bogin, Yehudi Wyner, Ward Davenny, Tong-Il Han, Frank Glazer, and Paul Jacobs; flutists Kyril and Rebecca Magg; clarinetist David Glazer; vocalist Susan Davenny Wyner. Concerts are held every Saturday afternoon during the season, on two Sunday afternoons, and there are two special children's concerts during the week. A lovely pastoral setting, relaxed atmosphere, enthusiastic audiences, and distinguished musicians producing fine music all add up to a very special feeling at Music Mountain!

For tickets and information write to: Music Mountain, Inc., Falls Village, Connecticut 06031. Telephone: (203) 824-7126.

For accommodations write to: Torrington Chamber of Commerce, 40 Main Street, Torrington, Connecticut 06790. Telephone: (203) 482-6586.

SILVERMINE CHAMBER MUSIC SERIES
New Canaan, Connecticut
Mid-July to mid-August for four Sunday evening concerts

Artists, sculptors, and ceramicists are in the majority at the Silvermine Guild of Artists during the weekdays, but on Sundays, there are not only artists, but musicians, and a large number of music devotees. The occasion is the Silvermine Chamber Music Series which has been held at the Guild since 1959. The Guild had been a cultural focal point in the New

England area since 1922 and thus it was a natural evolution for it to sponsor and initiate the series. When the chamber music programs began, they were organized around performances given by the Silvermine Quartet—Paul Wolfe and Joseph Schor, violin; Jacob Glick, viola; and Alexander Kougell, cello. Later, a Silvermine Chamber Orchestra and Music School was added. The orchestra and school are no longer a part of the program, but the original Silvermine Quartet has been reunited and performed at the 1977 and 1978 series.

The programs are given on three or four Sunday evenings and include seldom-heard works of the masters and some contemporary pieces. Mrs. Edith Grunewald has been director of the concerts from 1961 to 1977, and although there are no artists in residence, many musicians return each year for the series. Some of these have been Francisco Aybar and Murray Perahia, piano; Keith Wilson and Stanley Drucker, clarinets; Walter Trampler, viola, Julius Baker and Paul Boyer, flutists, and Robert Bloom, oboe.

Performances are held in the 300-seat Gifford Auditorium at the Silvermine Guild. The atmosphere at the concerts is relaxed and cordial, as demonstrated by an open invitation to the audience to meet the performers after the concerts and to wander through the art galleries at the Guild.

For information write to: Silvermine Chamber Music, c/o Silvermine Guild of Artists, 1037 Silvermine Road, New Canaan, Connecticut 06840. Telephone: (203) 966-5617.

For accommodations write to: New Canaan Chamber of Commerce, 24 Pine Street, New Canaan, Connecticut 06840. Telephone: (203) 966-2004.

YALE CONCERTS IN NORFOLK
Norfolk, Connecticut
Mid-June to the last week in July for six weeks

New England's musical traditions are rich, varied, and of long duration, and Norfolk has been a part of those traditions for almost eighty years. The Whitehouse, and later the Music Shed were the very special retreats and scenes of performances of the world's greatest artists and composers as early as 1899. The Norfolk Concerts were the inspiration and creation of the Battell and Stoeckel families (Carl Stoeckel was a well-known patron of music in Norfolk) who had a keen interest in the arts, and as a result, sponsored musical events on their lovely estate. Composers received commissions for their works played at the concerts, and the Litchfield County Choral Union, a local singing group, was a focal point in the season's programming. Jean Sibelius, Josef Hofmann, Victor Herbert, Sergei Rachmaninoff, Fritz Kreisler, Vaughan Williams, and Alma Gluck are a few of the many great artists and composers who were guests at the Music Shed. In 1941, the Yale University Summer School of Music became a sponsor of the concerts.

The programming for the concerts features chamber music ranging from early baroque to contemporary, and usually one performance of a choral work is presented by the Litchfield County Choral Union. The artists for these concerts are drawn from the in-residence faculty members at the Yale Music School and include Keith Wilson, artistic director, Arthur Weisberg, Ruth Laredo, Robert Nagel, Thomas Nyfenger, John Swallow, and the Tokyo String Quartet. The Yale School of Music enrolls fifty students of advanced musical attainments for a six-week intensive study of chamber music. During the season a few recitals are given by the students and are open to the public without charge.

The Ellen Battell Stoeckel Estate, the site of the Norfolk Concerts, is located in the northwest section of Connecticut in a region dotted with beautiful lakes, mountains, and verdant forests. The estate with over sixty acres has handsomely laid-out gardens and picnic areas which provide a rural and yet elegant setting for the musical event. The Music Shed within its grounds has seating for 1,000 patrons and is considered an acoustical marvel. Today's audience may still expect the finest chamber music performed by artists of the highest calibre just as they did at the turn of the century!

For tickets write to: Yale in Norfolk, Yale School of Music, 96 Wall Street, New Haven, Conn. 06520. Telephone: (203) 436-1342. After June first: "Yale in Norfolk" Battell Stoeckel Estate, Norfolk, Connecticut 06058. Telephone: (203) 542-5537.

For accommodations write to: Chamber of Commerce of Northwest Connecticut, 40 Main Street, Torrington, Connecticut 06790. Telephone: (203) 482-6586.

AMERICAN MUSIC FESTIVAL
Washington, District of Columbia
April and May on Sunday evenings

Postcards, movies, newspapers, and television have made Washington's famous buildings, monuments, and personalities familiar to everyone. Among these well-known landmarks is the National Gallery of Art of the Smithsonian Institute, one of the finest museums in the world with masterpieces of European and American paintings and sculpture. This famous gallery also plays host to the American Music Festival, a series of free concerts which were initiated in 1943 by Richard Bales, and are held every Sunday evening in the months of April and May in the East Garden Court, which accommodates 500 people.

Performances include chamber music, recitals, and choral music written by American composers from the eighteenth century to present day. Hundreds of world premieres and first Washington performances have taken place since its first season, and many composers have written especially for these festival series. Some of the composers whose works have been performed are Aaron Copland, Samuel Barber, George Crumb, Robert E. Helps, Howard Hanson, Walter S. Huffman, Burrill Phillips, Ned Rorem, and Richard Wernick.

The principal ensemble is the National Gallery Orchestra with Richard Bales as director and conductor. Invited guests who have appeared at the festival are Richard Becker, Anthony Newman, and Wayne Smith, pianists; Stephen Stalker and Lloyd Smith, cellists; Bruce Berg and Cordula Rosow, violinists; Rheta Smith, oboist; John Dexter, violist; and Diane Gold, flutist.

The combination of great art and fine music could make a visit to the National Gallery during April and May a very special Sunday outing.

For information write to: American Music Festival, National Gallery of Art, Washington, D.C. 20565. Telephone: (202) 737-4215.

For accommodations write to: Washington Area Convention and Visitors Association, 1129 20th Street N.W., Washington, D.C. 20036. Telephone: (202) 857-5500. Or: Chamber of Commerce of Washington, D.C. 20036. Telephone: (202) 857-5900.

INTER-AMERICAN MUSIC FESTIVAL
Washington, District of Columbia
First week in May for ten days

The Inter-American Music Festival celebrated its twentieth birthday in 1978 with a very impressive record. During its life span, it has premiered over 300 works by Latin American, Canadian, and United States composers! The festival started as a result of the imaginative planning of Guillermo Espinosa, then head of the music division of the Pan American Union. Espinosa brought together the best musicians from South and North America with the purpose of providing a cultural exchange between the Americas and giving composers and artists of the Western Hemisphere an opportunity to have their music performed. In the early days, the emphasis was almost entirely on the presentation of new works, but recently the focus has shifted to the twentieth-century music which deserved to be heard again, as well as presenting a new work at each concert. The festival is produced under the auspices of the Inter-American Music and Arts Foundation in cooperation with the Organization of American States, the Library of Congress, and the John F. Kennedy Center for the Performing Arts. Harold Boxer is general director. The Festival Orchestra is composed of professional musicians with invited guest conductors and soloists. Other orchestras and ensemble groups are invited to participate and have included the National Symphony of Washington, the Louisville Orchestra, Eastman Philharmonic, National Symphony of Mexico, Peabody Symphony Orchestra, Dorian Wind Quintet, and the Baltimore Symphony Orchestra. Guest conductors have included Carlos Chavez, Sergiu Comissiona, Guillermo Espinosa, Howard Hanson, Karel Husa, Jorge Mester, and Jose Serebrier; and artists, Per Brevig, Carl Gerbrandt, Antonio Jeronimo Menezes, Caio Pagano, Hilde Somer, Paula Seibel and Paul Zukofsky.

The list of composers who have had their works premiered is long, impressive, and representative of many countries in the Western Hemisphere—Henry Brant, Roque Cordero, Aurelio De La Vega, Morton Feldman, Alberto Ginastera, Louis Jorge Gonzales, Yannis Ioannidis, and Elie Siegmeister to name a few.

The 1977 festival commemorated the ninetieth anniversary of the birth of Heitor Villa-Lobos, Brazil's great composer (1887-1959). Not only did the festival feature music of the famous musician, but the concert was conducted by Mario

Tavares of Brazil and honored two great Brazilian women—Mme. Arminda Villa-Lobos, widow of the composer, and Bidu Sayao, Brazil's acclaimed soprano. Mme. Sayao was celebrating the fortieth anniversary of her Metropolitan debut.

The 1978 season programming had wide appeal as it included performers of many generations. Carlos Chavez, the seventy-nine-year-old Mexican composer, conducted the world premiere of his work, Concerto for Trombone, and later that season, twelve-year-old guitar virtuoso, Daniel Baquero Jimenz from Colombia presented a guitar symposium with Carlos Barbosa-Lima.

The concerts include symphonic, chamber, and folk music, and even dance concerts. Performances are held in the Concert Hall in the John F. Kennedy Center for Performing Arts seating 2600 patrons, as well as other facilities and performing halls—the Library of Congress, State Department Auditorium, Coolidge Auditorium, and the Hall of the Americas. Admission to the concerts is free.

Washington, D.C. can be a fascinating historical and political adventure for the resident or visitor, and with the Inter-American Music Festival, it provides a very rewarding musical experience. It is the best opportunity to keep abreast of what is happening in contemporary music in the Western Hemisphere.

For information and complimentary tickets write to: Inter-American Music and Arts Foundation, P.O. Box 23717, L'Enfant Plaza, Washington, D.C. 20024. Telephone: (202) 755-1933.

For accommodations write to: Washington Area Convention and Visitors Association, 1129 20th Street, N.W.; Washington, D.C. 20036. Telephone: (202) 857-5500.

BACH FESTIVAL OF WINTER PARK
Winter Park, Florida
Last week in February for two days

Applause, admission tickets, and a harpsichord at Winter Park were not in the thinking of Boston-bred music devotee and public benefactor, Mrs. Charles Sprague-Smith. She was the genteel power behind the Bach Festival for nearly two decades. Starting as a vesper service in 1935 under the direction of Dr. Christopher O. Honaas, the festival became the concern of Mrs. Sprague-Smith in 1937, and by sheer determination she gathered the necessary funds, recruited musicians, and ran the festival in the style she felt appropriate. She insisted there be no applause, that the choir be chosen as much for their reverence as for their voices, that the instrumentalists be restricted to a violinist and pianist and that only the music of Bach be performed. In keeping with her frugal New England background, she felt that a harpsichord would be too expensive and insisted instead that thumbtacks be stuck in the hammers of the small upright on stage to simulate the harpsichord's tinkling effect!

The Bach Festival still maintains its high standards of performances, but it has changed since Mrs. Sprague-Smith's day. The programs today include not only Johann Sebastian Bach's works, but large choral masterpieces of Brahms, Beethoven, Haydn, Purcell, and Bruckner; the festival is extended to two full days; the size of the Bach Festival Choir has increased to 130 voices, and a full orchestra is used along with a variety of instrumentalists. The music director and conductor since 1966 has been Dr. Ward Woodbury. He directs the Bach Festival Orchestra drawn from members of the Florida Symphony Orchestra and the Bach Festival Choir which includes selected singers from Central Florida communities and qualified students from Rollins College. Guest soloists who have appeared over the years are Joanna Simon, Carole Bogard, John Cheek, Hilda Harris, Stanley Kolk, Thomas Paul, Sandra Walker, Susan Davenny Wyner, and John Aler.

The festival is at Rollins College campus in Winter Park, Florida. The concerts are performed in Knowles Memorial Chapel which was built in 1932 and seats 600. Considered one of the most beautiful buildings in Florida, with its rare works of art, stained glass windows, and wood carvings, as the setting for the concerts it is indeed worthy of the occasion.

For tickets and information write to: The Bach Festival of Winter Park, Rollins College, Box 2731, Winter Park, Florida 32789. Telephone: (305) 646-2233.

For accommodations write to: Chamber of Commerce of Winter Park, 150 N. New York Avenue, Winter Park, Florida 32790. Telephone: (305) 644-8281.

NEW COLLEGE MUSIC FESTIVAL
Sarasota, Florida
June for three weekends

In 1927, John Ringling selected Sarasota as the winter quarters for his famous Barnum and Bailey circus. The attraction is without equal as "The Greatest Show on Earth." In 1965, Paul C. Wolfe, violinist and professor of music at New College in Sarasota, started the New College Music Festival. Its high calibre performances are also without equal as the only festival of national scope in the State of Florida.

Inspiration for the event came from Professor Wolfe and Dr. Arthur R. Borden, chairman of the Humanities Division of New College, as well as from an enthusiastic and supportive local community. Wolfe's goals were twofold: to offer a school in a teaching environment with the finest faculty-artists in residence and with students of exceptional talent from well-known music schools in the country and to present a first-rank music festival.

The festival provides full symphonic concerts, but the main emphasis is on chamber music. Each concert is varied and adventuresome in repertoire and ranges from baroque to contemporary offerings. The resident ensemble is the New College String Quartet with Paul C. Wolfe and Anita Brooker, violinists; Kenneth Stalberg, violist; and Robert Battey, cellist. There are six major concerts with faculty-artists performing in ensembles and as soloists with the orchestras, and Paul Wolfe as the conductor. There are also several free-admission concerts given by the students. The faculty is composed of distinguished artists who are members or former members of famous ensembles thoughout the country. Some of these performers have been Leonid Hambro, pianist; Robert Bloom, oboist; Raphael Hillyer and Walter Trampler, violist; Julius Baker, flutist; Ronald Leonard, cellist; Richard Burgin, James Buswell, and Joseph Silverstein, violinists; Richard Stoltzman and Keith Wilson, clarinetists; and Robert Nagel, trumpet. The faculty members offer students, who total 120 each season, an intensive three-week study with master classes, ensemble instruction, and performance experience.

The 1978 season was a memorable one for the audience as they welcomed three great regulars: Joseph Silverstein, concertmaster for the Boston Symphony Orchestra; Ronald Leonard, principal cellist for the Los Angeles Philharmonic; and Richard

Stoltzman, world-renowned clarinetist. All three were stars and received standing ovations, cheers, and foot-stamping approval from fellow colleagues in the orchestra!

Concerts are held on the campus of New College in the acoustically-fine Van Wezel Performing Arts Hall. Designed by Frank Lloyd Wright architects, it seats 1776 concertgoers. Student concerts are held in the New College Music Room, a lovely wood-paneled room built by Charles Ringling, and at the student center.

Sarasota has been blessed with sunshine and surf, art museums, circuses, and sports; but now it can also rightfully boast of a fine and successful music festival and school.

For tickets and information write to: New College Music Festival, 5700 North Tamiami Trail, Sarasota, Florida 33580. Telephone: (813) 355-2116.

For accommodations: Sarasota Chamber of Commerce, 1551-2nd Street, Sarasota, Florida 33577. Telephone: (813) 955-8187.

MISSISSIPPI RIVER FESTIVAL
Edwardsville, Illinois
Mid-June to mid-August for nine weeks

A full-time tent manager, one of the few left in the world who was trained in the old tradition of the circus, assures the audience that the "show will go on" at the Mississippi River Festival. The "show" in this case takes place on the eighteen-acre grounds of Southern Illinois University campus in Edwardsville, under a big white tent weighing over seven tons. With a seating capacity of 1,931, the tent has a special suspension system which provides an unobstructed view for an additional 15,000 patrons called "star gazers" who sit on the lawn to hear the concerts. And if there is ever a sign of bad weather, the tent manager and crew are on hand to put their skills to work and see that things run smoothly.

The Mississippi River Festival was organized in 1969 as a joint effort of Southern Illinois University and the Saint Louis Symphony Society, and since 1975, the University has had full sponsorship. The Saint Louis Symphony Orchestra is in residence during the summer and is the main ensemble. Many concerts are conducted by Leonard Slatkin and Gerhardt Zimmerman. Billed as "family entertainment," the season provides diversified musical programming with symphonic concerts, chamber music, a contemporary entertainment series with folk, jazz, blues, and ragtime entertainers. Other festival offerings have included dance companies, theatrical performances, films, art, crafts, and sculpture exhibits. Guest artists who have appeared in the classical series have included Daniel Majeske, Peter Serkin, Ruth Slenczynska, Abby Simon, André Watts, and Fred Zlotkin; and such ensemble groups as the Giovanni String quartet, Juilliard Quartet, and the Saint Louis Woodwind Quintet; and dance groups like the Phyllis Lamhut Dance Company, Nikolais Dance Theatre, and the Kathyrn Posin Dance Company. The contemporary artists series have featured Tex Beneke and his orchestra, Arlo Guthrie, Bob Hope, Gordon MacRae, Linda Ronstadt, Boz Scaggs, Fred Waring and many more.

In response to the educational needs of the area, the festival in recent years has added a Summer Dance Institute and a Summer Music Institute. These programs offer workshops during the summer varying from one to four weeks and are designed to benefit the student and professional alike.

For tickets write to: Mississippi River Festival, Box 37, Southern Illinois University at Edwardsville, Edwardsville, Illinois 62026. Telephone: (618) 692-3294.

For accommodations write to: Edwardsville Chamber of Commerce, Post Office Box 568, Edwardsville, Illinois 62025. Telephone: (618) 656-7600.

RAVINIA FESTIVAL
Chicago, Illinois
Last week in June to the second week in September
for eleven or twelve weeks

"Everywhere I look I see Renoirs!" said Paul Hindemith when he first saw the natural setting of Ravinia Park in 1961. Perhaps if he had seen the 36-acre park during a concert with 15,000 patrons, he would not have considered it the quiet rural picnic atmosphere so typical of the Impressionist painter. Ravinia, a major festival with a colorful and impressive history, has one of the longest, largest, and most varied seasons of any summer festival in the country. Originally, the land bought in 1902 was to be used as an amusement center to stimulate business for the railroads, but it was soon taken over by the Ravinia Corporation with the purpose of "bringing good music to the North Shore." As the Ravinia Opera, its "Golden Years of Opera" were between 1919 to 1931 when the greatest singers in the world performed on its small wooden stage. Lucrezia Bori, Mary Garden, Yvonne Gall, Giovanni Martinelli, Rosa Raisa, Elizabeth Rethberg, Tito Schipa and Virgilio Lazzari are a few of the many outstanding vocalists who made musical history at Ravinia. Those were the days when thirty-six different operas were presented during the ten-week season, with performances seven nights a week.

There were a few hazards and inconveniences with those outdoor productions. As many patrons had the long ride back to Chicago on special trains, the producers made concessions and staged *Carmen* without the first act and included only the "Flower Song." They cut *Aida* and "lopped" *Lohengrin!* And Mario Chamlee, the noted American tenor, once sang to the pitch of a train passing by the outskirts of the park! Suffering financial difficulties during the Depression, the opera company was forced to close for four years. In 1936 an association of local dignitaries and residents officially created the Ravinia Festival and thus established a permanent summer home for the Chicago Symphony Orchestra.

Considered a "total musical experience," Ravinia during its eleven-week season has a wide variety of entertainment, including orchestral and chamber music, opera in concert version, pops, jazz, theater, ballet, young people's programs and master classes. Usually the scheduling format is seven or eight weeks of classical and popular music, one week of ballet and one week of theater. There are performances every night during the season. James Levine, music director since 1972, conducts many of the programs and also has shared the podium with such renowned conductors as Ernst Arnsermet, Franz Allers, James Conlon, Arthur Fiedler, Josef Krips, Andre Kostelanetz, Seiji Ozawa, Michael Tilson Thomas, Sixten Ehrling, William Steinberg, and Edo de Waart. Ravinia continues its tradition of engaging the world's finest solo artists such as vocalists Eileen Farrell, Regine Crespin, Claudine Carlson, Sherrill Milnes, Jessye Norman, Leontyne Price, Elisabeth Schwarzkopf, Ragner Ulfung, and Beverly Wolff; pianists John Browning, Christoph Eschenbach, Van Cliburn, Alicia de Larrocha, Peter Serkin, and André Watts; violinists Mayumi Fujikawa and Samuel Magad. For the popular music concerts, outstanding artists are engaged such as Harry Chapin, Judy Collins, Ella Fitzgerald, Benny Goodman, Arlo Guthrie, Pete Seeger, Neil Sedaka, Bobby Short, and Frank Zappa.

The Chicago Symphony Chorus under the direction of Margaret Hillis plays an important role in the festival as the chorus appears in the opera and choral presentations.

Dance groups have included the Joffrey Ballet, Martha Graham Dance Company, Merce Cunningham and Dance Company, and Pilobolus Dance Theatre.

Performances are held at the Ravinia Pavilion. A unique structure built in 1950, it has a fan-shaped roof which "floats" on a row of slender steel columns at the outer edge so the view is unobstructed for 3,500 patrons inside. There is additional lawn seating outside for 15,000 patrons. For more intimate musical events—recitals, chamber music and theater performances, the 923-seat Murray Theatre is used.

For tickets write to: Ravinia Festival Association, 22 West Monroe Street, Chicago, Illinois 60603. Telephone: (312) 782-9696.

For accommodations write to: Chicago Visitors and Convention Bureau, 332 S. Michigan Avenue, Chicago, Illinois 60604. Telephone: (312) 922-3530.

PENDLETON FESTIVAL SYMPHONY SUMMERFEST
Pendleton, Indiana
Mid-June to the first week in August for six weeks

George Daugherty, Jr., music director of the Pendleton Festival Symphony, might be considered an "early bloomer," having founded the "Summerfest" in 1975 when he was only eighteen years old! Daugherty's musical career started at the age of four in Pendleton with piano lessons, which were soon followed with musical productions in his backyard in which he would cast his neighborhood playmates (his friends acted in pantomime while records played the songs). He believes that his idea for the festival began when he wanted to conduct Prokofiev's *Peter and the Wolf* with the high school band, but there were not any available string players. Although he had never seen the complete score or the music, he rewrote the work using the instruments at hand. Soon after, the band with Daugherty on the podium performed the piece for an audience of 200! In 1976, at age twenty, he made his professional opera debut with Metropolitan opera soprano, Roberta Peters.

Maestro Daugherty has never felt that his age has been a detriment to his career, but he has received unusual reactions. When violin virtuoso, Eugene Fodor, came to the festival for the first time in 1977, he asked Daugherty how old he was. Daugherty said, "I'm twenty-one." Fodor, then twenty-seven, was so taken aback and surprised, he gasped, "When's the next plane back to Colorado?" At the concert a few days later, both young men proved to have expertise far beyond their years!

The Pendleton Festival Symphony is comprised of eighty-five young professional musicians (average age is twenty-three) including those from the symphony orchestras of Chicago, Denver, Saint Paul, Grand Rapids, Baltimore, and Indianapolis, as well as from music schools and conservatories — Eastman, Cleveland Institute of Music, Indiana University, Juilliard, Oberlin, and many others. Guest soloists are invited each year and have included vocalists Judith Mattox Boone, Wayne Harris, Roberta Peters, William Reynolds, and Carol Sweeney-Sparrow; violinist Eugene Fodor; and pianist Elizabeth Edmundson. The 1978 season welcomed the entire Harvard Glee Club, the nation's oldest collegiate chorus, with mezzo-soprano Rosalind Elias.

The festival season offers four or five programs during the six-week period, and the usual format includes an evening of symphonic works with vocal or instrumental soloists, a fully staged opera, a "Mostly Mozart" event, and an evening of light classics. Concerts are held in the 1600-seat Paramount Theatre in Anderson (ten miles north of Pendleton and forty miles northeast of Indianapolis), at the First United Methodist Church, and at Falls Park in Pendleton.

For tickets and information write to: Pendleton Festival Symphony Summerfest, 421 East State Street, Pendleton, Indiana 46064. Telephone: (317) 778-3009.

For accommodations write to: Anderson Chamber of Commerce, 100 W. 11th Street, Anderson, Indiana 46015. Telephone: (317) 642-0264.

ROMANTIC MUSIC FESTIVAL
Indianapolis, Indiana
Late April for eight days

Spring in Indianapolis means the "Indy 500" and the Romantic Music Festival! Presenting rarely performed and forgotten music of the nineteenth century, the festival, under the guidance, inspiration, and directorship of Frank Cooper, is exposing concertgoers to unknown composers such as Jeral, Gliere, Gade, Alkan, Busoni, Raff, Lumbye, Dreyschock, Spohr, and Chausson. And they love it! Cooper, a brilliant pianist, scholar, and recording artist in his own right, has possibly the world's best collection of nineteenth-century sheet music, and he used this as the basis for founding the festival in 1968.

Symphonic and choral works, chamber music, concerti, and ballet have been performed by Jordan College students as well as talented guest performers and orchestras. Among the orchestras appearing at the festival have been the Butler University Symphony Orchestra, the Indianapolis Symphony with Izler Solomon, the Louisville Orchestra with Jorge Mester, and Fort Wayne Chamber Orchestra. Some of the great interpretive artists of the romantic period who have made their appearances are pianists Jorge Bolet, Balint Vazsony, Frank Cooper, Malcolm Frager, Gunnar Johansen, and Raymond Lewenthal; violinists Aaron Rosand and Charles Treger; violoncellists Jascha Silberstein and James Kreger; organist Marilyn Mason; and vocalist Mary Ellen Pracht. All performances are held in the 2200-seat

Clowes Memorial Hall which is on the campus of Jordan College of Music at Butler University.

Definite and comprehensive program notes are provided for each performance, and in keeping with the nineteenth-century motif and atmosphere, some programs have settings reminiscent of the romantic period and artists are dressed in costumes of the nineteenth century. The concerts strive to evoke a bit of the magic and mystery of the romantic era, and some of the programs have flashes of showmanship. In one concert in 1968, Gunnar Johansen, the pianist, was performing Franz Liszt's *Dance of Death.* Johansen and a $15,000 Imperial Grand Piano were on a platform at stage level while the orchestra played, unseen, down below! That same year pianist Raymond Lewenthal played Adolph Von Henselt's *Concerto* in complete darkness, except for the light on the music stand. "Considering the demoniac fury of Lewenthal's playing, it was spooky!" reported one reviewer.

The Romantic Festival has not only received national acclaim, but it has gained international recognition: in 1974, Arnhem, Holland started a romantic music festival patterned after the one at Butler University. It is a unique example of the cultural flow in reverse — Indianapolis to Europe!

For tickets write to: Romantic Music Festival, Butler University, Clowes Memorial Hall, 4600 Sunset, Indianapolis, Indiana 46208. Telephone: (317) 924-1267.

For accommodations write to: Chamber of Commerce of Indianapolis, 320 N. Meridan Street, Indianapolis, Indiana 46202. Telephone: (317) 635-4747.

CORNELL COLLEGE MUSIC FESTIVAL
Mount Vernon, Iowa
Late April or early May for three days

Hospitality, community spirit, and support have been a tradition with the Cornell College Music Festival since its beginning in 1898. In the early days there were receptions and pre-concert suppers; John Klimo, a station agent for the Chicago and North Western Railway, entertained members of the orchestra with his famous "buttermilk parties" (a euphemism for a stronger beverage than buttermilk!). Characteristic of the feeling of relaxation and cooperation that has prevailed over the years is an incident in 1914, when Mlle. Jennie Defau, a well-known soprano in the Chicago Opera Company, arrived in Mount Vernon in time for her scheduled appearance at the festival—only to find she was in Mount Vernon, Ohio! Her absence from the right Mount Vernon was quickly covered by members of the orchestra who gave solo recitals.

The festival was started in 1898 by Charles H. Adams, director of the Cornell College Conservatory of Music, when he organized an oratorio society of ninety voices for concerts. He received such praise and support from townspeople that word spread and soon the festival with its fine performers became known as the musical oasis of the Midwest. For nearly forty years (1903 to 1942), Dr. Frederick Stock, a talented musician and conductor of the Chicago Symphony, appeared yearly at the festival with the orchestra. After his death in 1942, the Chicago Symphony Orchestra continued its association with the festival until 1963. Since that time the Saint Louis Orchestra, Indianapolis Symphony Orchestra, Kansas City Symphony Orchestra, and the Minneapolis Symphony Orchestra have appeared at the festival.

Presently, the programming includes guest artists and ensembles along with the Cornell Chamber Orchestra directed by Daniel Greeting. The performances include symphonic works, chamber music, vocal and instrumental recitals, and jazz concerts. The guest artists over the years make an imposing list: vocalists Adele Addison, Phyllis Bryn-Julson, Marilyn Horne, Cornell McNeil, Judith Raskin, Martial Singher, Jennie Tourel, and William Warfield; pianists David Burge, Byron Janis, Eugene Istomin, Yvonne Loriod, Oliver Messiaen, Roslyn Tureck, and Ralph Votapek; cellist Janos Starker; and saxophonist Sonny Rollins.

Mount Vernon, Iowa, seventeen miles east of Cedar Rapids, is the home of Cornell College. The festival is held on the campus grounds in King Chapel. Built in 1875, the historic chapel is in American Gothic style and made of yellow dolomite limestone quarried in the area around Mount Vernon. The auditorium seats 1000 patrons and has a 65-rank Moeller pipe organ and A.L. Killian carillon bells—(86 English and Flemish bells which can be played from the organ or from a special console).

The festival has been an important musical event in Iowa for over three-quarters of a century and can justifiably claim much credit for its contribution to Iowa's musical growth and interest.

For information write to: Cornell College Music Festival, Cornell College, Mount Vernon, Iowa 52314. Telephone: (319) 895-8811.

For accommodations write to: Cedar Rapids Chamber of Commerce, 127 3rd Street, N.E., Cedar Rapids, Iowa 52401. Telephone: (319) 364-5135.

MESSIAH FESTIVAL
Lindsborg, Kansas
Easter week for eight days

"The Oberammergau of the Plains" is the name give the Messiah Festival in Lindsborg, Kansas. A group of Swedish immigrants in the 1860s settled in the Smoky Valley region of central Kansas and brought with them a love of music and community. Under the leadership of Dr. and Mrs. Carl Swensson in 1882, the first Messiah Festival began. With an unpretentious beginning using the voices of local townspeople, the Bethany Oratorio Society has grown to more than 400 singers, including Bethany College students and faculty, and a seventy-member symphony orchestra. During Easter week there is an eight-day celebration with performances of Bach's *Saint Matthew's Passion* on Good Friday, two performances of Handel's *Messiah,* and many other concerts throughout the week.

The concerts are presented by the Bethany Community Symphony Orchestra, the Bethany College Choir and the Bethany Oratorio Society and includes choral works, oratorios, and solo recitals. Guest professional soloists are invited to attend, and over the years concertgoers have seen Barbara Hocher, Mallory Walker, D'Anna Fortunato, Wayne A. Mitchell, Elizabeth Patches, Ronald Corrado, Robert Johnson, and Susan von Reichenbach, as well as many members of the music faculty at Bethany College. Dr. Elmer Copley, professor of voice at Bethany College, conducts the Bethany College Choir and David J. Higbee, a member of the faculty, conducts the orchestra for the festival. All concerts are held on the campus of Bethany College in Presser Auditorium which seats 1,800 patrons.

Easter week in Lindsborg is an involvement for the community and a very meaningful experience for visitors, as over the years audiences have numbered in the hundreds of thousands and each season the enthusiasm and numbers increase!

For information and tickets write to: Messiah Festival Ticket Office, Bethany College, Lindsborg, Kansas 67456. Telephone: (913) 227-3312.

For accommodations write to: Lindsborg Chamber of Commerce, 110 South Main Street, Lindsborg, Kansas 67456. Telephone: (913) 227-3706.

LOUISIANA STATE UNIVERSITY FESTIVAL OF CONTEMPORARY MUSIC
Baton Rouge, Louisiana
Early spring for one week

Harmonic partials, multiple sonorities, twelve-tone serialism, non-retrograde rhythms, and electronic synthesized sounds are all a part of the musical vocabulary of the Festival of Contemporary Music. The festival began at Louisiana State University in 1944 under the inspiration of Helen Gunderson, a professor emeritus of composition and theory at the university, and established itself as one of the first contemporary music festivals in the country. The programs include twentieth-century music—some "classic," some avant garde, and some conservative. All of the artistic organizations on campus are utilized for the festival . . . opera, choruses, symphony orchestra, chamber music groups, dance ensembles and the electronic studio. Compositions of the students and faculty are always included in the performances. Occasionally a guest symphony orchestra or contemporary ensemble group are invited to perform. These have included the New Orleans Philharmonic, the Concord String Quartet, and the Baton Rouge Symphony.

World premieres are an important part of the festival, and composers are invited to attend the festival, give seminars and talks to complement their new work. Some of the featured guest composers have been Violet Archer, Carlos Chavez, Milton Babbitt, Jacob Druckman, Ernst Krenek, Hermann Reutter and Elie Siegmeister. Otto Luening, noted American composer and pioneer in the electronic music field, appeared at the festival in 1976 to tell about the beginning of electronic music and to give students insights into his musical thinking. Patrons, performers, and critics recall a "Vintage Year-1977" when over thirteen compositions were premiered at the festival; the majority of them composed by faculty and students at the university.

Concerts are held on the campus of Louisiana State University, and are free and open to the general public. The Union Theater, with a seating capacity of 1300, is used for symphonic presentations, and the Union Colonnade and University Theater, each with a seating capacity of 500, are used for smaller ensemble presentations. Dinos Constantinides, festival chairman and accomplished violinist, and a prolific composer who has had many compositions premiered at the festival, also founded a concert series called "New Times." Now the student body at the University can hear the sounds of the future all year around as contemporary music is kept alive on campus.

For information write to: Louisiana State University, School of Music, Baton Rouge, Louisiana 70803. Telephone: (504) 388-3261.

For accommodations write to: Baton Rouge Chamber of Commerce, P.O. Box 3988, Baton Rouge, Louisiana 70821. Telephone: (504) 387-1400.

BAR HARBOR MUSIC FESTIVAL
Bar Harbor, Maine
First week in August for nine days

Maine is abundantly rich in festivals — the Maine Lobster and Seafood Festival in Rockland, the Potato Blossom Festival in Fort Fairfield, the Fisherman's Festival in Boothbay Harbor, and in Bar Harbor, each summer, the Bar Harbor Music Festival. The picturesque coastal community welcomes many visitors each summer, many of whom wish to explore Acadia National Park and to enjoy the beauties of the sea, mountains, lakes, and forests that have made this region world-famous as a summer resort. Cruises and many cultural activities are offered during the summer. In this climate it is highly appropriate to have a music festival.

In 1964, violinist Francis Fortier started the Bar Harbor Festival. The first years, the event was all-encompassing and included films, art exhibits, concerts, and lectures in many different locations throughout the city. In recent years, it has limited its season's activities to six musical concerts within a nine-day period. The programs feature instrumentalists and vocalists in recital with the repertoire ranging from traditional to light classics. Some of the artists have been Francis Fortier, artistic director; Stephanie Anne Jutt, Doris Coleman, Judith Olson, Victoria Villamil and Walter Ponce. The majority of the concerts are held in the College of the Atlantic Auditorium and one concert is performed at the Sewall Campground at Acadia National Park.

As it is almost impossible to receive advance information on the festival, it is best to check with the Chamber of Commerce once in Bar Harbor to determine if your holiday coincides with the festival activities.

For information write to: Bar Harbor Festival Corporation, Municipal Building, 93 Cottage Street, Bar Harbor, Maine 04609. Telephone: (207) 288-3393.

For accommodations write to: Bar Harbor Chamber of Commerce, Municipal Building, 93 Cottage Street, Bar Harbor, Maine 04609. Telephone: (207) 288-3393.

BAY CHAMBER CONCERTS
Rockport, Maine
July and August for eight Thursday evenings

"Most good things in Maine seem to move and change slowly: seasons, weather, people. The growth of the Bay Chamber Concerts to their present stature has been no different." These words of Andrew Wolf are spoken by a man with experience; in 1961, already an accomplished pianist at the age of sixteen, he and his fifteen-year-old brother Thomas, a talented flutist, founded the Bay Chamber Concerts. Music had been a very important element in the life of the Wolf family and in the life of Rockport since the early 1920s when the Curtis Institute, under the patronage of Mrs. Louise Bok of Philadelphia, started holding its summer teaching sessions in Rockport. The summer school of the Curtis Institute attracted such famous artists as Max Aronoff, Josef Hoffmann, Josef and Rosina Lhevinne, Gian-Carlo Menotti, Eugene Ormandy, Gregor Piatigorsky, Carlos Salzedo, Bidu Sayao, Elisabeth Schuman, Efrem Zimbalist, and many others. Andrew and Thomas Wolf's grandmother, Mme. Lea Luboshutz, noted violinist, made a tremendous musical contribution to the Rockport colony, as did their uncle, Boris Goldovsky.

The Curtis Institute sessions continued during the summer months until World War II. Its departure left a cultural void of major magnitude. The Wolf boys were aware of the historic contribution music had made to the culture of Rockport and set about filling that void by presenting the Bay Chamber Concerts.

Concerts are given on Thursday evenings and include works from the baroque period up to the present, but the primary emphasis is on the music of the great masters. The world-renowned Vermeer Quartet is in residence during the summer, and includes Shmuel Ashkenasi and Pierre Menard, violin; Jerry Horner, viola; and Marc Johnson, cello. Invited guests have included such notables as Giorgio Ciompi, violin; Leslie Parnas, cello; Artur Balsam, Peter Serkin, Andrew Wolf, Vladimir Sokoloff, pianists; Thomas Wolf, flute; Larry Guy, clarinet; and Nobuko Imai, viola.

In the first years, concerts were held at the Saint Thomas Parish House in Camden, but in 1973, the series moved to its new home in the Rockport Opera House. Built in 1891, the house played host to traveling theatrical companies for nearly twenty years, after which it was used for town meetings and social affairs. It was in danger of being demolished in 1971, but a "Save the Opera House" campaign was successful in rescuing the historic building. Now remodeled, it has a colorful interior, fine acoustics, and is a most appropriate setting for 400 patrons to hear chamber music at its best.

The Bay Chamber Concerts with Andrew Wolf, artistic director, have felt a strong commitment to the Maine community, and as a result, in 1974 expanded its programs into a year-round series taking performances to the schools and communities around the state, by featuring Maine composers, and by awarding musical scholarships to talented Maine music students.

And as for the summer music enthusiast who wishes to find the Bay Chamber Series, remember Rockport is "Down Maine" when one is traveling up the east coast of the state. Just ask a native.

For information write to: Bay Chamber Concerts, Inc., Post Office Box 191, Camden, Maine 04843. Telephone; (207) 236-2419.

For accommodations write to: Camden, Lincoln, Rockport Chamber of Commerce, Post Office Box 246, Camden, Maine 04843. Telephone: (207) 236-4404.

BOWDOIN COLLEGE SUMMER MUSIC FESTIVAL
Brunswick, Maine
Last week in June to the last week in July for five weeks

Bowdoin College, founded in 1790, has an impressive legacy numbering among its graduates some distinguished citizens in American history: Henry Wadsworth Longfellow, Admiral Robert E. Peary, Nathaniel Hawthorne, President Franklin Pierce, and explorer Donald B. MacMilan. Bowdoin isn't resting on its laurels; today it strives to make musical history as well, with a fine summer music festival, a summer School of Music, and a Contemporary Music Festival held in the fall.

Both the festival and the music school were formed in 1965 by Lewis Kaplan in order to give sixty or more serious young students of high school and college age a concentrated program of musical instruction, practice, and performance.

The Aeolian Chamber Players with music director Lewis Kaplan, violin; Jacob Maxin, piano; Thomas Hill, clarinet; and Ronald Thomas, cello are the basic ensemble for the festival. This group is known for its musical excellence and extensive repertoire of both traditional and contemporary works. They function as faculty members for the school and give concerts every Thursday evening during the season with other guest artists of international reputation. Some of these fine musicians have been Martin Canin and Emanuel Ax, pianists; Robert Davidovici, Michael Rabin, and Setsuko Nagata, violinists; Leslie Parnas and David Soyer, cellists; Paul Doktor, violinist; and Erich Graf and David Whiteside, flutists; Robert Beckwith is director.

There are several student recitals during the season and Saturday evening is reserved for "Star Night" when an outstanding student is featured in a performance. There are also two evenings featuring twentieth-century music. The 1978 season welcomed composer-in-residence, George Crumb, who performed some of his compositions.

If a visitor misses the summer series held in the 300-seat Kresge Auditorium on the Bowdoin campus, he should make a point of attending the two-day Contemporary Music Festival in October. Different sounds are heard issuing from the auditorium—perhaps Japanese temple bells, tuned crystal goblets, suspended cymbals, maraca or crotales. Many interesting compositions have been premiered by the Aeolian Chamber Players. Since the festival's first year in 1965, the works of many famous composers have had their first performances here, including those of Luciano Berio, Elliott Carter, George Crumb, Donald Erb, William Duckworth, George Rochberg, and Elliot Schwartz. It is here that Bowdoin is making musical history!

For information write to: Bowdoin College Summer Music Festival, Department of Music, Bowdoin College, Brunswick, Maine 04011. Telephone: (207) 725-8731.

For accommodations write to: Brunswick Area Chamber of Commerce, 59 Pleasant Street, Brunswick, Maine 04011. Telephone: (207) 725-8797.

KNEISEL HALL
Blue Hill, Maine
First week in July to the middle of August for seven weeks

Blue Hill, a small community off the coast of Maine, abounds in natural beauty and elegant cultural traditions. Remaining relatively unexploited and undiscovered, it is tucked away from the main stream of activity between tourist-filled Bar Harbor and Penobscot Bay. It has the great distinction of hosting one of the finest chamber music schools in the nation. Franz Kneisel, eminent violinist, friend of Johannes Brahms, teacher, and a pioneer of chamber music in the United States, founded the famous Kneisel Quartet in 1885. He headed up the string department of the Institute of Musical Art, today known as the Juilliard School of Music, and beginning in 1902, Kneisel brought his best music pupils to his vacation retreat in Blue Hill, Maine. These teaching holidays evolved into the first chamber music school in the country. Kneisel's goal was to provide for students in the beautiful setting of Blue Hill, an opportunity to experience an intensive training in the art of ensemble playing under the direction of the finest teachers.

In this cultural milieu some of the world's greatest musicians taught, studied, and performed at Blue Hill — Lillian and Joseph Fuchs, Louis Kaufman, Fritz Kreisler, Jacques Gordon, Gregor Piatigorsky, Eudice Shapiro, and Willem Willeke, to name a few. Kneisel's dear friend, Felix Kahn built Kneisel Hall in 1922, thereby assuring a permanent site for the concerts and the school.

After Kneisel's death in 1926, his daughter, Marianne, directed the school for thirty-seven years. Upon her death in 1963, Leslie Parnas, distinguished cellist, inherited this prestigious and established musical tradition and became artistic director. He has maintained the highest level of teaching, has further involved the concerts and the school in the community life at Blue Hill, and updated the facilities at the school to accommodate a total of sixty students.

Concerts are scheduled for every Wednesday evening and Sunday afternoon, and are performed by members of the faculty and an occasional guest artist. There are also many student concerts given without charge to the public during the last half of the musical season. Some of the many talented artist-faculty in recent years have been Giorgio Ciompi, Claudia Erdberg, Raphael Hillyer, Artur Balsam, Edmund Battersby, Ani Kavafian, Barbara Stein-Mallow, Gregor Piatigorsky, Leslie Parnas, Andrew Wolf, Roman Totenberg, Karen Tuttle, Mischa Michakoff, Rya Garvusova and Walter Trampler. Guest artists have been James Buswell, Lorin Hollander, and the Vermeer Quartet.

Kneisel Hall, where the concerts are held, is perched on the slope of the Blue Hill Mountains—a dramatic view with the Blue Hill Bay stretched out at its feet. The hall has exceptionally fine acoustics and as the 180 seats within the hall are always in demand, some concertgoers sit outside on the lawn area and enjoy the music from that vantage point.

The glorious past is very much alive in Blue Hill, for Kneisel Hall has had an extraordinary place in the history of chamber music in this country, and the artists and the concerts they give perpetuate this strong musical tradition. In some summer retreats the air is filled with the screech of sea gulls, the pounding surf, or the rumble of motorboats, but at Kneisel Hall there are the melodic strains of Bach, Beethoven, and Bartok.

For information and tickets write to: Mrs. Ruth Kneisel, Post Office Box 251, Castine, Maine 04421. Telephone: (207) 326-8294.

For accommodations write to; Chamber of Commerce, Post Office Box 267, Ellsworth, Maine 04615. Telephone: (207) 667-5584.

MONTEUX MEMORIAL FESTIVAL
Hancock, Maine
First week in July to mid-August for six weeks

"Learning to play the entire orchestra" is what some of the students claim is happening at the Monteux Domaine School for Conductors and Orchestra Players in Hancock, Maine. It is a relaxed, non-competitive atmosphere where fifty or more musicians go in the summer for various reasons: young aspiring musicians wish to learn the techniques of conducting; professional musicians wish to sharpen their conducting skills; music teachers wish to learn about teaching conducting; and others to brush up on their orchestra skills.

Pierre Monteux, world-renowned conductor, opened a conducting school for young people at his home in Hancock, Maine.

Upon his death in 1943, his wife continued operating the school and the Pierre Monteux Memorial Foundation was formed to perpetuate the maestro's work. Charles Bruck is director and headmaster, and a number of Monteux's former pupils and other professional musicians are on hand as faculty. The students and the faculty give orchestra and chamber music concerts every Wednesday and Sunday evenings during the season and present works ranging from Mozart to Ives.

The school is situated on sixty-eight acres of farmland amidst woods and haystacks in a quiet rural setting, and concerts are held in the 350-seat Hall at Hancock Corner. The small community of Hancock is off Route One a few miles east of where most of the tourists travel, so be on the lookout for a small unpretentious sign, hung from a weatherbeaten wood frame announcing, "Pierre Monteux Memorial Domaine School." You will have arrived at your destination and are in for a delightful musical treat.

For information write to: Pierre Monteux Domaine School, Hancock, Maine 04401. Telephone: (207) 422-3931.

For accommodations write to: Ellsworth Chamber of Commerce, Post Office Box 267, Ellsworth, Maine 04605. Telephone: (207) 667-5584.

CASTLE HILL FESTIVAL
Ipswich, Massachusetts
Early July and August for five weekends

"The music of the zither, the flute and the lyre enervates the mind," so said Publius Ovidius Naso in 25 B.C. Music director Thomas Kelly, the festival's musicians and dancers, and those who attend the Castle Hill Festival series would disagree with the opinion of this Roman poet. The festival boasts of producing some of the finest early baroque music in the country and uses the instruments mentioned by Ovid, as well as the kummerhorn, violini, recorders, and a harpsichord. Not only is the music uplifting, but so is the location of the festival—one of the most outstanding and beautiful estates in the East, Castle Hill, built by Chicago plumbing magnate, Richard T. Crane, in the 1930s. Used only as a summer residence, the great Georgian-style mansion rises majestically over a long flawless beach on the Atlantic Ocean in Ipswich, thirty-five miles north of Boston.

Musical offerings were first held in 1950 when the Castle Hill Foundation was organized to preserve the estate and to sponsor the events. The festival offically opened in 1972, and in 1978, Castle Hill was entered into the National Register of Historic Places.

The festival offers a series of ten or more weekend concerts with emphasis on the authentic baroque and Renaissance music. Tom Kelly, music director and conductor, seeks to reproduce the authentic sounds of the period and uses early versions of such instruments as violin, oboe, and cello — stringed instruments are played on gut rather than wire; horns are valveless and of a smaller bore than modern horns; and often, a group of six to twenty musicians are conductorless. In this way, the director produces music in the manner he believes composers of Bach's era would have wished. A resident festival orchestra formed in 1977 includes musicians from all over the country and Europe. Many performers return each year; some of these include mezzo-soprano Jantina Noorman, member of the Musica Reservata in London; Frank Hoffmeister, tenor; Jane Bryden, soprano; Jeffrey Gall, counter tenor; Jean Lamon, violinist; John Gibbons, harpsichord; Marion Verbruggen and Philip Levin, recorders; and Stephen Hammer, oboist.

Programs include opera, chamber music, recitals, and dance, and are held in the outside "Casino" area with seating for over 1,000 or inside "The Barn," a large Italian Renaissance structure with a country feeling, seating 500. Other festival offerings are Sunday afternoon concerts for the elderly, educational programs with an Early Dance and Music Week, workshops with programs such as seventeenth- and eighteenth-century outdoor music, an orchestra symposium, and a children's early dance week.

For tickets and information write to: Castle Hill Festival Concerts, Box 283, Ipswich, Massachusetts 01938. Telephone: (617) 356-4070, or (617) 484-4172.

For accommodations write to: Ipswich Chamber of Commerce, Ipswich, Massachusetts 01938. Telephone: (617) 356-3231.

NEW MARLBOROUGH MUSIC CENTER
(Red Fox Music Camp)
New Marlborough, Massachusetts
First week in July to mid-August for five weeks

Red Fox Music Barn was named after the red fox weathervane atop the turn-of-the-century barn in New Marlborough, Massachusetts. The original barn situated on a beautiful seventy-five-acre farmland site in the southern Berkshires in western Massachusetts, has been thoroughly renovated, for even the cow stalls were removed to make room for the concert hall area and for offices. Here each summer 150 students, aged twelve years and over, come from all over the country to participate in a six-week camp program which includes chamber and orchestral work, theory, sightreading, private lessons, and an opportunity to perform at student concerts. In 1949, Isabelle Sant' Ambrogio, concert pianist and educator, started the Red Fox Music Camp, and seven years later formed the New Marlborough Chamber Players who function as the faculty at the camp. The New Marlborough Chamber Players are musicians from major orchestras, universities, and conservatories all over the country, and are the performing artists at the concerts. Some of the faculty have been violinists Martha Caplin, Kathryn Caswell, and Lazar Gosman, director of the Leningrad Chamber Orchestra; pianists John Covelli, Malcolm Frager, Isabelle Sant' Ambrogio, director of New Marlborough Chamber Players, and William Workinger; cellists Melissa Meell, Richard Naill, and John Sant' Ambrogio; violists Martha Brownell, Diann Jezurski and Jesse Levine; clarinetists Jerry Kirbride and Harry Noble.

Concerts are held every Saturday night during the season in the barn with a seating capacity of 200. The programs include chamber music ranging from baroque compositions to the more contemporary, and the ensembles vary in size from duets and trios to quartets and quintets. The 1977 season featured the Primavera String Quartet, an all-woman group who that same year had won the Naumberg Chamber Music Competition in New York. Their repertoire included fifteenth-century music played from manuscripts as well as a quartet by Shostakovitch.

For ticket information write to: New Marlborough Music Center, New Marlborough, Massachusetts 01230. Telephone (413) 229-7790.

For accommodations write to: Great Barrington Chamber of Commerce, 362 Main Street, Great Barrington, Massachusetts 01230. Telephone: (413) 528-1510.

SOUTH MOUNTAIN CONCERTS
Pittsfield, Massachusetts
First week in July to the second week in September
for ten Saturday evenings

"The Fairy godmother of chamber music" was the name affectionately given to Mrs. Elizabeth Sprague Coolidge, founder of the South Mountain concerts, by musicologist W.W. Cobbett. Mrs. Coolidge, American patroness of Music, accomplished pianist and composer, created the Berkshire String Quartet in 1916 so she might give musicals in her home. Two years later, she started the South Mountain concert series with the help of Willem Willeke, a world-renowned cellist and one of the original musicians in a string ensemble. The purpose of these concerts was to present outstanding chamber music ensembles and soloists of the day and to perform music of contemporary composers. Many new works were commissioned by and dedicated to Mrs. Coolidge by such composers as Ernst Block, Sir Edward Elgar, Manuel de Falla, Roy Harris, Paul Hindemith, Ottorino Respighi, Arnold Schoenberg, Ernst Toch, and Anton Webern. These early festivals included competition for chamber music work and provided exposure and stimulus for the composers. Mrs. Coolidge also built at the top of South Mountain, a house, a concert hall, and four cottages for members of the Berkshire String Quartet. The 600-seat concert hall, named Music Temple, has superb acoustical qualities and provides a unique setting with a dramatic view of the beautifully forested Berkshire hills in western Massachusetts.

The South Mountain concerts continued, though sporadically, between 1928 and 1949. When Willem Willeke died in 1950, his widow, Sally, succeeded him as artistic director and has continued to maintain the traditions and high standards of this festival. The concerts are given on Saturdays during the summer season and engage outstanding soloists and ensembles. Past seasons have welcomed Dame Myra Hess, William Kapell, Ruth Laredo, and William Masselos, pianists; Fritz Kreisler, Alexander Schneider, Joseph Silverstein, and Efrem Zimbalist, violinists; Jan De Gaetani, Reri Grist, Leontyne Price, Leonard Warren, vocalists; Beaux Arts Trio, Budapest String Quartet, Guarneri String Quartet, Juilliard String Quartet, and New York Camerata.

An important concept inaugurated in 1955 by Mrs. Willeke was the Young Audience Concerts. Thirty or more concerts are given in one season, and over 20,000 school children in western

Massachusetts and New York have been introduced to and enjoyed chamber music concerts.

South Mountain Concerts has had a long and distinguished musical history, and yet it is planning for the future by offering interesting programs and by educating and stimulating a new generation of potential concertgoers with its Young Audience Concerts.

For tickets write to: South Mountain Concerts, South Mountain Association, Box 23, Pittsfield, Massachusetts 01201. Telephone: (413) 443-6517.

For accommodations write to: Central Berkshire Chamber of Commerce, 107 South Street, Pittsfield, Massachusetts 01201. Telephone: (413) 499-4000.

TANGLEWOOD
(Berkshire Music Festival)
Lenox, Massachusetts
First week in July to the last week in August for nine weeks

The Berkshire Music Festival, best-known as "Tanglewood," is the oldest major summer music festival in the country and one of the most esteemed summertime musical events in the world. Tanglewood is situated in Lenox, a beautiful small New England town in the Berkshire Hills of western Massachusetts. The first concert series was presented in 1934 by the Berkshire Symphony Orchestra, composed of sixty-five members of the New York Philharmonic Orchestra. The concerts were immediately successful, and the organizers of the series began a search for an established symphony orchestra. In 1936, they invited the Boston Symphony Orchestra under the leadership of Serge Koussevitzky to participate in a festival. Also at that time, the association between the orchestra and Tanglewood officially began when Miss Mary Aspinwall Tappan and her niece, Mrs. Gorham Brooks, gave the Tappan family Berkshire estate, Tanglewood, to the orchestra—thus the Boston Symphony Orchestra established its summer residence at Tanglewood.

The activities at Tanglewood are multifaceted and extensive; at the core is the Berkshire Music Festival, a nine-week concert season featuring the Boston Symphony Orchestra with Seiji Ozawa as music director since 1973. Programs include orchestral works with vocal and instrumental soloists, choral works, and opera in concert form. The Boston Symphony concerts are

held Friday and Saturday evenings and Sunday afternoons. On Saturday mornings, there is often an open rehearsal with a modest entrance fee which benefits the Boston Symphony Orchestra's pension fund. In addition to this, there are weekly "Prelude" concerts which precede the Friday evening concerts; "Pops on Parade"—an evening with Arthur Fiedler; a popular artists series; and "Tanglewood on Parade," a day-long celebration combining all of the orchestras at the Music Center. The grand finale is an evening performance of Tchaikovsky's 1812 Overture, complete with cannon and fireworks.

Mention of some of the many fine guest artists who have performed at Tanglewood in recent years indicates the pronounced high level of musical standards: conductors Aaron Copland, Leonard Bernstein, Colin Davis, Eduardo Mata, Jorge Mester, Neville Marriner, Seiji Ozawa, André Previn, William Steinberg, and Michael Tilson Thomas; pianists Alicia de Larrocha, Christoph Eschenbach, Gary Graffman, Horatio Gutierrez, Martin Isepp, Lili Kraus, Peter Serkin, and André Watts; violinists Mayumi Fujikawa, Joseph Silverstein, Isaac Stern, and Pinchas Zukerman. Some of the renowned vocalists have been Judith Blegen, Maureen Forrester, Benjamin Luxon, Seth McCoy, Jessye Norman, John Shirley-Quirk, Jon Vickers, and Benita Valente.

In addition to presenting the festival, Tanglewood offers a very comprehensive school, the Berkshire Music Center. Started in 1940 by Dr. Serge Koussevitzky, and under the direction of the Boston Symphony Orchestra and Gunther Schuller, the Center is designed to give advanced music students and fully accomplished young musicians an opportunity to perfect their skills by working with the best professional people in their respective fields. The teaching staff consists of guest artists and various members of the Boston Symphony Orchestra, who, along with the students, offer numerous concerts which are performed in the Theater Concert Hall and for which a modest fee is charged. A subscription as a "Friend of Music at Tanglewood" includes admission to all Berkshire Music Center performances. The list of graduates at the Center is most impressive: Leonard Bernstein, Phyllis Curtin, Lawrence Foster, Lorin Maazel, Leontyne Price, Seiji Ozawa, Thomas Schippers, Michael Tilson Thomas, and many more.

A high point of the Center's activities each August is the Festival of Contemporary Music sponsored by the Center and the Fromm Music Foundation at Harvard. This internationally acclaimed "festival within a festival" looks forward and backward in its programming, as it presents neglected contemporary works often overlooked today, as well as new music, some of which is commissioned by the Center. Frequently, participating composers are invited to take part in the festival by giving seminars and lectures.

All Boston Symphony concerts are held in the Shed, an enormous wood and steel structure designed by Eliel Saarinen and Joseph Franz in 1938 with open sides and an excellent amplifying system. Inside the Shed there is seating for 5,090 festival-goers; and there is additional space outside on the vast lawn where thousands more may listen to the concerts. Tanglewood has 210 acres of unspoiled scenic beauty and many concertgoers find it perfectly suited for preconcert strolls and picnics.

Many writers, statesmen, and well-to-do New Yorkers and Bostonians were attracted to the peace and beauty of Tanglewood in the mid-1850s. Nathaniel Hawthorne, inspired by the wooded countryside and lovely trees, named the area Tanglewood, and there planned his book, *Tanglewood Tales*. Though many years have passed, the area still retains its charm and is now enjoyed by multitudes of music lovers and musicians who make their pilgrimage annually to this very special place.

For information write to: Until first week in June: Festival Ticket Office, Symphony Hall, Boston, Massachusetts 02115. Telephone: (617) 266-1492. After the first week in June: Festival Ticket Office, Tanglewood, Lenox, Massachusetts 01240. Telephone: (413) 637-1600. (For a Friends of Music at Tanglewood membership, write to: Development Office, Symphony Hall, Boston, Massachusetts 02115.)

For accommodations write to: Lenox Chamber of Commerce, Main Street, Lenox, Massachusetts 01240. Telephone: (413) 637-3646.

WORCESTER MUSIC FESTIVAL
Worcester, Massachusetts
Late October for two weekends
with five or six concerts

The Worcester Music Festival is back home again! After an absence of forty-six years, many of the concerts are again being performed at Mechanics Hall where the festival staged its first musical event. As the oldest annual musical festival in the country, it has many interesting tales to tell of its illustrious past. Started as a choral festival in 1858, the opening concert by the Worcester County Musical Institute charged twenty-five cents admission and attracted a total of 170 patrons! The years that followed, 1866 to 1897, were called "the first golden age" as Carl Zerrahn, the music director, established the "starring system" and engaged such great artists as Jenny Lind, Nellie Melba, and Lillian Nordica. He also shared the podium with Victor Herbert and Anton Dvorak. Between 1925 and 1943, another musical giant emerged: Albert Stoessel, a conductor greatly respected and beloved by his colleagues and audiences. He is credited with not only engaging the best soloists available, but for giving relatively unknown artists an opportunity to be heard. Maestro Stoessel brought full operatic productions to the festival, championed the cause of American music, and premiered many compositions during his brilliant tenure.

The festival, sponsored by the Worcester County Music Association includes oratorios, large choral works, opera, symphonic works with solo vocalist and instrumentalist, and pops. The Worcester Chorus, composed of qualified vocalists in the area, still is an integral part of the festival and performs each season. A Concert for Young People is also included, with Dr.

David Epstein, conductor of the Worcester Orchestra. Since 1944, guest conductors and symphony orchestras have been invited to the festival, and in recent years have included the Buffalo Philharmonic Orchestra with Michael Tilson Thomas, Boston Symphony Orchestra with Seiji Ozawa, Baltimore Symphony Orchestra with Sergiu Comissiona, Detroit Symphony Orchestra with Paul Paray, Philadelphia Orchestra with Eugene Ormandy and the Rochester Philharmonic Orchestra with David Zinman. Guest artists have included Peter Binder, Ruben Dominquez, Rosalind Elias, Malcolm Frager, Eugene Fodor, Robert Merrill, Roberta Peters, Jessye Norman, Peter Nero, Joseph Silverstein, and André Watts.

Concerts are given in two facilities now: the 2,852-seat Memorial Auditorium, and the original site, the Mechanics Hall. Built in 1857 with Roman Corinthian colonnades, the Mechanics Hall was once the center of the city's artistic, political, and educational life. Lectures were given by Emerson, Mark Twain, and Thoreau, and concert recitals by Paderewski and Caruso! For many years the Hall was used as a roller skating rink, but in 1977 it was completely renovated. The Hall seats 1500 people and is blessed with exceptionally fine acoustics. Once again concertgoers may admire the elaborate interior with its large paintings and lovely murals and be reminded of the "golden" history of the festival while they are enjoying top flight musical performances.

For information write to: Worcester County Music Association, Memorial Auditorium, Worcester, Massachusetts 01608. Telephone: (617) 754-3231.

For accommodations write to: Worcester Chamber of Commerce, 350 Mechanics Tower, Worcester, Massachusetts 01608. Telephone: (617) 753-2924.

ANN ARBOR MAY FESTIVAL
Ann Arbor, Michigan
Late April or early May for four days

Stability, continuity, and a consistently high caliber of musicality have been the hallmarks of the Ann Arbor May Festival since its founding in 1894 by the University Musical Society. The Boston Festival Orchestra was the principal ensemble from 1894 to 1905, followed by the Chicago Symphony Orchestra for thirty-one years. In 1936, the Philadelphia Orchestra became the nucleus for the concerts with Leopold Stokowski conducting. The following year, Eugene Ormandy, music director and conductor began his long tenure which has continued to the present day. The program format, remaining virtually unchanged since its beginning, presents music with full orchestra, shared with solo vocalists or solo instrumentalists and a large choral program accompanied by the orchestra. The University Choral Union, a 300-voice chorus made up of Ann Arbor students and residents has been the principal choral group of the festival since 1894. The tradition of engaging great prima donnas and solo virtuosos started in the early days with singers Ernestine Schumann-Heink, Tito Schipa, John McCormack, and Lillian Nordica; violinists Mischa Elman and Albert Spalding; pianists Josef Lhevinne and Ossip Gabrilowitsch.

Most recently the list of performers has included conductors Igor Stravinsky, Howard Hanson, Aaron Copland, and John Pritchard; pianists Van Cliburn, André Watts, Rudolf Serkin, Arthur Rubinstein, Glenn Gould, and Gary Graffman; violinists Jascha Heifetz, Isaac Stern, and Yehudi Menuhin; and singers Marilyn Horne, Jessye Norman, Beverly Sills, Leontyne Price, Regine Crespin, Joan Sutherland, Jerome Hines, Dietrich Fisher-Dieskau, Martina Arroyo, Montserrat Caballé, and many others.

The concerts are held in the 4,177-seat Hill Auditorium on the campus of the University of Michigan. The University hosts a year-around schedule of cultural events which builds in intensity until the May Festival, which is representative of the best in musical entertainment. This excellent, long-established festival lives up to its motto, *"Ars longa, vita brevis."*

For tickets write to: University Musical Society, Burton Tower, Ann Arbor, Michigan 48109. Telephone: (313) 665-3717.

For accommodations write to: Ann Arbor Chamber of Commerce, 207 E. Washington St., Ann Arbor, Michigan 48108. Telephone: (313) 665-4433.

MEADOW BROOK MUSIC FESTIVAL
Rochester, Michigan
Last week in June to the last week in August for ten weeks

Tucked into a sloping sylvan corner of the former estate of Mrs. John Dodge, widow of the automobile manufacturer, is the site of the Meadow Brook Music Festival. Called the Baldwin Memorial Pavilion, the fiberglass shell is placed within a natural amphitheater, and under a simple pitched roof, 2,200 patrons may sit and listen to concerts. An additional 5,000 concertgoers may sit on the slopes around the pavilion. Before the concerts, entire families are encouraged to come early and picnic — it's alfresco in the lovely surroundings of flowers, lawn, and trees. The property, donated by Mr. and Mrs. Alfred Wilson, became the site of the festival when it officially opened in 1964.

Presenting a full spectrum of musical entertainment — symphonic and chamber music, operas in concert form, jazz, pops, ballet, children's concerts, and matinee open rehearsals, Meadow Brook Concerts are performed Thursday through Sunday evenings each week during the ten-week season. The Detroit Symphony Orchestra makes its summer home at Meadow Brook. Sixten Ehling was its music director for the first ten years, followed by Aldo Ceccato for a three-year period, who was then followed by Antal Dorati in 1977. Neville Marriner is the present music director. Guest conductors are invited to share the podium each season — and the list is most impressive — Aaron Copland, André Kostelanetz, Erich Leinsdorf, Charles Munch, Seiji Ozawa, André Previn, Klaus Tennstedt, Michael Tilson Thomas, and Roger Wagner, to name a few. Internationally acclaimed guest artists appearing over recent years have included: Claudio Arrau, Van Cliburn, Mary Costa, Philippe Entremont, Maureen Forrester, Anna Moffo, Jessye Norman, Jan Peerce, Itzhak Perlman, Michael Rabin, Isaac Stern, Peter Serkin, Yo-Yo Ma, Paul Plishka, and André Watts. The pops evenings have engaged stars such as Ella Fitzgerald, Tony Bennett, Chuck Mangione, Cleo Laine, Oscar Peterson, Arlo Guthrie, and Pete Seeger. The festival points with pride to the number of interesting compositions that have been commissioned and premiered at the festival. Roger Sessions, Carlos Surinach, Ulysses Kay, Ernest Krenek, Lester Trimble and Yusif Lateef have all had their compositions introduced at Meadow Brook!

For tickets write to: Meadow Brook Music Festival, Oakland University, Post Office Box 705, Rochester, Michigan 48063. Telephone: (313) 377-3100.

For accommodations write to: Rochester Chamber of Commerce, 812 N. Main Street, Rochester, Michigan 48063. Telephone: (313) 651-6700.

NATIONAL MUSIC CAMP
Interlochen, Michigan
*Last week in June to the last week in August
for eight weeks*

Called the "Daddy of Them All," the National Music Camp in Interlochen, Michigan qualifies as the largest music camp for young people in the country. Dr. Joseph E. Maddy had a dream of providing better music for young people, and he set about attaining his goal in 1928. With his friend, Thaddeus Giddings, a public school music supervisor, they found an unpretentious rustic hotel in the Michigan woods. Funds were so limited that they took the campsite in exchange for a five-year boarding contract. Maddy gathered 115 students, a staff of qualified music teachers, and soon thereafter, the camp-school became a reality. The camp was an immediate artistic success, but financially it struggled many years to survive. However, the camp celebrated its fiftieth anniversary in 1977 and now enrolls more than 1,500 students from forty-six states and twenty-two foreign countries who utilize over four hundred buildings within its beautiful campus! The fiftieth anniversary season had a memorable concert when composer Howard Hanson conducted the world premiere of his newest composition, *Sea Symphony* for chorus and orchestra.

George C. Wilson, music director and principal conductor of the National Music Camp, has held both positions for over thirty-five years and has seen many alumni of the camp, now holding outstanding music positions throughout the world, return to Interlochen in the summer as part of the faculty.

Students who attend the eight-week session range from eight years of age to college level, and are exposed to concentrated studies in such fields as drama, dance, art, and music. Not only do they receive instruction from a well-trained faculty numbering over 200, but they are exposed to the talents of some of the world's leading professionals who are invited guests each summer. Some of these fine artists in past seasons have included Dave Brubeck, Aldo Ceccato, Van Cliburn, the Concord String Quartet, Benny Goodman, Howard Hanson, Margaret Hillis, Bob Hope, Stan Kenton, Ani Kavafian, Jessye Norman, Helen Quach, and Robert Shaw.

The public is invited, often without charge, to the concerts presented during both the day and the evening. In the past season, over 350 concerts performed by the faculty and the students were offered during the eight weeks. The programs are varied, and range from band concerts, jazz, pops, opera, operetta, chamber music, orchestral concerts to drama, dance, and instrumental or vocal recitals. Depending upon the size of the productions, concerts are held in one of the three principal facilities: Corson Auditorium, a fine concert hall seating 1,000; the Kresge Auditorium, an outdoor theater with a covered roof and seating for 4,000; and the Bowl, an uncovered amphitheater with seating for 4,000.

The community of Interlochen is located in northern Michigan, fifteen miles southwest of Traverse City in the heart of the state's vacationland. The campus with its 1,200 wooded acres dotted with virgin pines and two large inland lakes, is a woodland sanctuary away from the distractions of city life. The atmosphere is ideal for young musicians to produce beautiful music and for concertgoers to hear young talent and professional musicians at their best.

For information write to: National Music Camp, Interlochen, Michigan 49643. Telephone: (616) 276-9221.

For accommodations write to: Traverse City Chamber of Commerce, Post Office Box 387, Traverse City, Michigan 49684. Telephone: (616) 947-5075.

FESTIVAL OF CONTEMPORARY MUSIC
Las Vegas, Nevada
Late October for one week

Ravel and roulette go hand-in-hand in Las Vegas, for here is a fine festival of contemporary music in the gambling and show business capital of the world. Virko Baley, a Ukraine-born pianist-composer and faculty member of the University of Nevada, started the festival in 1971. The university sponsored the musical event and placed emphasis on bringing "new contemporary" music to Las Vegas, as well as commissioning new works. Initially, a group of local musicians made up the orchestra, but as the festival grew, the local ensemble developed into a professional group, the Las Vegas Chamber Players, and guest performers and composers are invited to the festival.

Mr. Baley prides himself on his "eclectic programming of music of this century. We play music we believe in, and go out of our way to avoid specializing or being narrow ideolgically." In keeping with this philosophy, jazz-oriented composers such as David Baker and Eugene Kurtz have premiered their compositions at the festival. The list of world, United States, and western premieres is long and impressive. For example, during the past seasons Paul Chihara's *Kyrie-Sally Garden*, Virko Baley's *Partita for Trombone and Tape*, Bernard Rand's *Serenata 75b*, Alvin Epstein's *Levitation 74*, Netty Simon's *Songs for Jenny*, and Charles Lipp's *Infinite Gratitude* were presented for the first time. Composers-in-residence are an important ingredient for the festival, presenting lectures, recitals, demonstrations, workshops, and performances of their compositions. Among their numbers have been Luis de Pablo, Paul Chihara, Paul Zonn, Eugene Kurtz, Donald Erb, Roger Reynolds, Morgan Powell, and Bernard Rands. Guest ensemble groups have been TASHI, the San Francisco Contemporary Music Players, University of Illinois Contemporary Chamber Players, and Dharma-A Jazz Quartet. Guest artists have included conductors Ed London, Keith Humble, and Paul Polivnick; instrumentalists Bertram Turetzky, Paul Zonn, Christina Petrowska, and Miles Anderson. The university campus is not far from the famous bustling Las Vegas "Strip." The concerts held in the 2,000-seat Artemus W. Ham Concert Hall with its avant-garde recitals and contemporary presentations are in strong contrast to the 24-hour activity of Las Vegas' bright night excitement!

Write for information and tickets to: Contemporary Music Festival, Music Department, University of Nevada, Las Vegas, Nevada 89154. Telephone: (702) 739-3332.

For accommodations write to: Greater Las Vegas Chamber of Commerce, 2301 E. Sahara Avenue, Las Vegas, Nevada 89104. Telephone: (702) 457-4664.

NEW HAMPSHIRE MUSIC FESTIVAL
Center Harbor, New Hampshire
First week in July to mid-August for six weeks

Crystal-clear lakes, high mountains, and bracing climate have attracted people to the White Mountains Lakes Region of New Hampshire for years. In this dramatic setting the New Hampshire Music Festival adds to the charm of the area. It all began in the mid-1940s when Mrs. Heidy Speilter and Mr. and Mrs. J. Edward Kurth recruited an orchestra of New York musicians to play for their pleasure on Sunday afternoons. This became so enjoyable that people went out in boats on Lake Winnipesaukee to listen! By 1953, this informal arrangement became so popular that the festival was established to provide summer concerts by resident professional musicians for all the people in the communities in the New Hampshire Lakes Region.

The festival orchestra, composed of musicians from some of the country's leading symphony orchestras and music schools, is in summer residence at Plymouth State College. The Music Department at the College joins the thirty-four-piece orchestra to offer week-long workshops in choral and keyboard study. Thomas Nee, conductor and music director of the festival since 1961 offers programs of symphonic works and chamber music. Joel O. Johnson directs the 150-voice New Hampshire Festival Chorus which employs singers from 25 New Hampshire communities. Guest artists have included violinist Yoshiko Nakura; pianists Frank Glazer, James Bonn, and Anne-Marie Levine; flutist Leone Buyse; vocalists Frederick Johnson, Winthrop Buswell, and Rosanne Halloran.

Concerts are held in the evenings at various communities in the Lakes Region — Silver Hall in Plymouth; Gilford Middle High School in Gilford, and Interlakes High School in Meredith. In keeping with the New Hampshire Music Festival's theme of reaching new audiences in various locations, in 1975 a few members of the chamber music group who called themselves "Hutband," carried classical music to the heights by performing on the mountain slopes of 6,288-foot Mount Washington! They played chamber music at mountain shelters and huts. During the concerts, the lack of oxygen sometimes affected the wind players, and local insects came on the scene in force. The audience of backpackers lacked the dignity of a formal concert hall, but they responded to the music with great enthusiasm, and claimed they relished the chamber music in those simple wooden refuges. No doubt, a new audience!

Write for tickets to: New Hampshire Music Festival, Post Office Box 147, Center Harbor, New Hampshire 03226. Telephone: (603) 253-4331.

For accommodations information, write to: Lakes Region Chamber of Commerce, Laconia, New Hampshire 03246. Telephone: (603) 524-5531.

WHITE MOUNTAINS FESTIVAL OF THE ARTS
Jefferson, New Hampshire
Late June to mid-August for eight weeks

The White Mountains Festival of the Arts points with pride to the local townspeople, innkeepers, trustees, teachers, artists, musicians, dancers, and students who have made this co-operative venture such a success. The festival is held in the small community of Jefferson in the "north country" of New Hampshire and is blessed with a unique and beautiful setting within sight of the great White Mountains and the majestic Presidential Range with many peaks towering over 5,000 feet. In addition to the dramatic physical surroundings, the festival's performance site is on the grounds of the old Waumbek Inn, a historical attraction in itself, built in 1860.

The festival was organized by the members of a consortium of business, artistic, and educational organizations who thought that the area around Jefferson was ideal for a festival. The first season in 1972 included a series of ballets, concerts, workshops, clinics, and sculpture exhibits, and that format is used today.

Emphasis is on music with a wide popular appeal, and programming includes traditional classics, jazz, and folk music. Mr. John Goyette has been executive director since 1975 and some of the first-rate musical performers he has booked have been Dave Brubeck, Dizzy Gillespie, Benny Goodman, Keith Jarrett, Buddy Rich, John Sebastian, and Livingston Taylor as well as the Hartford Ballet, Preservation Hall Jazz Band, and the Monadnock Symphony. In addition to the musical offerings, there is a sculpture workshop and ballet instruction during the season.

The first few years, the musical events were held in a candy-striped tent on the grounds of the Waumbek Inn. In 1976, a plea was made for help in building a new stage and terracing the lawn around the inn. Many volunteers answered the call and constructed a permanent wooden pavilion which accommodates 900 festival-goers.

Visitors to the Granite State in the summertime should include not only the lovely resort areas around Lake Winnipesaukee, the notches of Franconia and Pinkham, but also the beautiful White Mountains area with its Festival of the Arts.

For information write to: White Mountains Festival of the Arts, Box 145, Jefferson, New Hampshire 03583. Telephone: (603) 586-4322.

For accommodations write to: Littleton Chamber of Commerce, Main Street, Box 105, Littleton, New Hampshire 03561. Telephone: (603) 444-2351.

WATERLOO SUMMER MUSIC FESTIVAL
Stanhope, New Jersey
Mid-July to mid-August for five weeks

A restored ghost town, nestled in the rolling hills and lakes of northern New Jersey, is the site of the Waterloo Summer Music Festival. During the American Revolution it was called Andover Forge and was the producer of most of the ammunition for the Continental Army. After the war, the English who settled in the region renamed it Waterloo Village to commemorate Wellington's defeat of Napoleon! Percival Leach and Louis Gualandi "rediscovered" the community in 1946 and brought the original character of the village to life through crafts, restoration of the buildings, and music. In 1968 they inaugurated the Music Festival and the Waterloo Foundation for the Arts.

Within the spacious grounds of the village and not far from the original eighteenth-century structures — the general store, steepled church, gristmill, potter's barn, and Stagecoach Inn — is a large circus tent used for the concerts. Brilliantly striped in green and white, the tent seats 3,000 patrons who listen to symphonic and chamber music during the festival. Following the five-week season, jazz, pops, and bluegrass concerts are presented.

Gerard Schwarz, music director since 1976, was co-principal trumpet player for the New York Philharmonic, but resigned in 1977 to be able to give more time to conducting, to the festival, and to the school. He founded the Waterloo Music School in 1976 which now enrolls 120 advanced music students. The students work closely with the faculty members, some of whom are cellist Frederick Zlokin; violinist Syoko Aki; pianists Kenneth Cooper and Samuel Lipman; and oboist Ronald Roseman. Much as does the Marlboro Festival in Vermont, Waterloo School strives for a strong musical interaction between the professional musicians and the talented young students. Concerts are given Thursday and Saturday evenings and Sunday afternoons.

The ninety-plus Waterloo Festival Orchestra is made up of students from the school, faculty members, and musicians from the ranks of the New York Philharmonic, New York City Opera, and the Metropolitan Opera Orchestra. In recent years guest soloists have been Byron Janis, Clamma Dale, Philippe Entremont, André Watts, Van Cliburn, Emanuel Ax, and Eugene Istomin.

Concertgoers recall with joy the concert in 1970 when Pablo Casals, the noted cellist and conductor, played Mozart's Symphony no. 41 with such brilliance, inspiration, and passion that the audience exploded with enthusiasm into a prolonged standing ovation. Afterwards the ninety-three-year-old maestro was heard chuckling and commenting in his modest way, "You might say that you heard a rather good performance."

For tickets write to: Waterloo Music Festival, Waterloo Village, Stanhope, New Jersey 07874. Telephone: (201) 347-4700.

For accommodations write to: Hackettstown Chamber of Commerce, 107 Moore Street, Hackettstown, New Jersey 07840. Telephone: (201) 852-1253.

NEW MEXICO MUSIC FESTIVAL AT TAOS
Taos, New Mexico
Third week in July to the last week in August for five weeks

The joy of making beautiful music in a unique and spectacular setting is one of the many appealing features of the New Mexico Music Festival at Taos. The establishment of the festival in 1978 came about by a series of curious events. Mark Camphouse, the festival's music director and conductor, intended to start a music festival in a town in the Black Hills of South Dakota. Changes in the University of South Dakota's music department caused Camphouse to reconsider the original site. He went to a Mobile Travel Guide to find a community suitable for a music festival, and at random selected Taos. He wrote to the Harwood Foundation in Taos, and the letter was directed to Noel Farrand, president of the Friends of American Music in Taos. Farrand immediately offered Camphouse a "home" for his proposed festival with the added enticement of the sponsorship by the Friends of American Music.

The New Mexico Music Festival offers to approximately one hundred students five weeks of intensive private lessons, master classes, public performances in small ensembles and with full orchestra, faculty lectures, and instruction in conducting, compositions, and music literature.

The faculty includes accomplished musicians with extensive backgrounds as soloists, and a combination of orchestral and ensemble players. The artist-faculty, numbering approximately twenty-two, work closely with the students and rotate positions in the orchestra so that students often progress to the first chair positions. Among the faculty are David Diamond, composer-in-residence; David Oppenheim, clarinetist; Patricia Black, Digby Bell, and Richard Cameron, pianists; Janet Ferguson, flutist; John Dewitt and Susan Enger, trumpetists; Kathleen Golding, oboist; Kenneth Wolfson, bassoonist; and Allan Kaplan, trombonist. The Delphi String Quartet, composed of Leslie Sawyer, Charles Hott, Carlene Stober, and Marion Froehlich, is an important part of the festival, as is also an experimental workshop featuring improvisational compositions under the direction of Richard Cameron.

The programs emphasize new or neglected American music, as well as the more familiar standard European works. During the five-week season, concerts are given five days a week with student and faculty recitals, and concerts on weekdays and Sundays. Full Festival Symphonic Orchestra concerts are reserved for Saturday evenings. Concerts are held in 275-seat Taos Community Auditorium located in the center of town.

The New Mexico Music Festival is distinguishing itself from other music-school festivals by the youth of its faculty, which lacks the "big names" of Tanglewood and Aspen, and by its emphasis on American music. With its unique and special geographical location, Taos has been known throughout the years as a haven for the visual arts; now, the New Mexico Music Festival is on hand, providing fine classical music as well.

For information write to: New Mexico Music Festival at Taos, Taos, New Mexico 87571. Telephone: (505) 758-8029.

For accommodations write to: Taos Chamber of Commerce, Drawer 1, Taos, New Mexico 87571. Telephone: (505) 758-3873.

SANTA FE CHAMBER MUSIC FESTIVAL
Santa Fe, New Mexico
First week in July to the first week in August for five weeks

"The greatest July 4, 1976!" recall residents in Santa Fe. The Santa Fe Chamber Music Festival hosted a grand Bicentennial celebration which began with a procession around Santa Fe's Plaza led by the Santa Fe Chamber Music group, followed by a community ecumenical service and concert in Saint Francis Cathedral with the Santa Fe Brass Choir, readings from Lao-Tzu, and a special blessing from the archbishop! The magic of this celebration is typical of Santa Fe's spirit. The festival began in 1973 in an area well-known to opera enthusiasts and is another musical event of quality offered during Santa Fe's summer. The festival strives to present varied programs — standard pieces along with unusual compositions rarely heard, of chamber music, solo recitals, and informal lecture-performances — to new audiences of varying backgrounds, some who seldom have an opportunity to hear chamber music.

Santa Fe, the oldest seat of government in the United States, still retains much of its original Spanish character, yet affects an interesting blend of Indian, Spanish, and Anglo cultures. There are many historic buildings which provide beautiful settings for the presentation of chamber music. The festival takes advantage of these settings by presenting concerts in such places as Saint Francis Cathedral, built in 1869, with seating for 500 and the auditorium in the Museum of New Mexico. Another very unique and special site is the 200-year-old adobe Santuario de Guadalupe where the altar bells are used in lieu of dimming lights to signal the end of intermission at a concert.

The festival also takes its programs on tour all over New Mexico and the Southwest and uses performing facilities at hand — plazas, churches, ranches, school auditoriums, and gymnasiums. In keeping with its goal of community involvement, one of its first concerts in 1973 was given on a Navajo Reservation, Window Rock in New Mexico, where the tribe was commemorating the fiftieth anniversary of the founding of the Navajo Tribal Council. The concert was so successful that the Santa Fe Chamber Music Festival has returned every year.

The festival's founder and artistic director, Alicia Schachter, is an accomplished pianist and performs frequently at the festival. The participating artists, all prominent musicians with major solo careers have included Claus Adam, Alfred Brendel, Bonnie Hampton, Paul Hersch, Mark Kaplan, Ani Kavafian, Heiichiro Ohyama, Sylvia Rosenberg, Leon Spierer, John Toth, Walter Trampler, Michael Webster, and the Vermeer Quartet. The American composers-in-residence have included Aaron Copland, William Schuman, and Richard Wernick. Special guest artists in recent seasons have been Maureen Forrester, Sheri Greenawald, and Philip Ruder.

Festival director Sheldon Rich feels that the challenge of each festival is "to try to create the atmosphere in which the special and unique can occur . . . the festival has now blossomed into a music program that extends throughout the state — to Indian reservations and small towns. We won't be satisfied until we've got all of New Mexico humming the 'Trout' Quintet."

For tickets and information write to: Santa Fe Chamber Music Festival, P.O. Box 853, Santa Fe, New Mexico 87501. Telephone: (505) 983-2075.

For accommodations write to: Santa Fe Chamber of Commerce, P.O. Box 1928, Santa Fe, New Mexico 87501. Telephone: (505) 983-7317.

CARAMOOR FESTIVAL
Katonah, New York
Mid-June to mid-August for nine weeks

Considered the most elegant and aristocratic annual festival in the New York area, Caramoor provides music as splendid as its surroundings. In Katonah, northern Westchester, less than two hours' driving time from New York City, Caramoor was the name given to the lavish Mediterranean-style country estate of the late Walter and Lucie Rosen. Music had been an important part of Caramoor since the 1930s when the Rosens gave private concerts for their friends in the mansion's lovely music room. Sometimes Mr. Rosen played the piano and Mrs. Rosen played her theremin, an electronic instrument invented by a Russian musician. Their keen interest in the arts and music led to the beginning of the festival in 1946.

One of the most beautiful areas on the estate is the open air Venetian Theater built around marble Greek and Roman columns brought from a fifteenth-century villa in Italy. It stands at one end of a sunken garden and has a stage large enough to accommodate a symphony orchestra and full-scale opera. There is seating for 1500 patrons under the stars . . . and in case of rain, canopies are set up alongside the theater. When the theater opened in 1958, concertgoers recall one of the most memorable and wet evenings at Caramoor; a downpour lasting for an hour and a half failed to dampen the spirit of the audience, as they knew the musical delight to follow. Marian Anderson sang the title role in Gluck's *Orfeo*. It was a brilliant performance, but it was the first and last time Miss Anderson sang that role!

An open air Spanish courtyard is used for more intimate musical offerings—small opera productions, chamber music, recitals, and children's programs. The courtyard is surrounded by the Caramoor House and provides 550 patrons with a charming setting for this special kind of presentation. Programs include symphonic works, chamber music, solo recitals, and in keeping with the tradition at the festival, rarely performed music and premieres are offered. Faure's *La Bonne Chanson,* Handel's *Semele,* and Cherubini's *Medea* have added interest to the season, as well as world and American premieres of Hugh Aitken's *Fables,* Benjamin Britten's *Curlew River* and *Prodigal Son,* and two children's operas, *Daughter of the Double Duke of Dingle* and *The Ballad of Bremen Band* by James Billing and Dennis Arlan.

The festival orchestra is comprised of members of the New York City Opera, Buffalo Symphony, and the Pittsburgh Symphony. Performers are drawn from the first rank of the active concert world and have included singers; Mary Costa, Charles Bressler, Beverly Sills, Brent Ellis, and Jessye Norman; instrumentalists, Gina Bachauer, Alicia De Larrocha, Micha Dichter, Garrick Ohlsson, Eugene Fodor, Philippe Entremont; and ensemble groups, TASHI, Beaux Arts Trio, Bach Aria Group, Tokyo String Quartet, and the New York Renaissance Band, to name a few. The Caramoor Festival Orchestra is conducted by Julius Rudel, musical director since 1964, and guest conductors have been Sir Alexander Gibson, and Brian Priestman. Concerts are held in the evenings on Saturday at 8:30 P.M., Sundays at 5:30 P.M., and children's concerts on Saturday mornings.

For ticket information write to: Caramoor Music Festival, Box R, Katonah, New York 10536. Telephone: (914) 232-4206.

For accommodations write to: Mount Kisco Chamber of Commerce, 295 Main Street, Mount Kisco 10549. Telephone: (914) 666-7525.

CHAUTAUQUA SUMMER MUSIC PROGRAM
Chautauqua, New York
Late June to the last week in August for nine weeks

Is it likely that such a diverse group as Susan B. Anthony, Thomas A. Edison, Marian Anderson, Arnold Schoenberg, Theodore Roosevelt, Admiral Richard E. Byrd, Amelia Earhart, and George Gershwin all have something in common? Yes, a visit to Chautauqua! Prominent people from many fields — scientists, writers, critics, politicians, artists, and religious leaders have been going to Chautauqua to attend lectures, lead discussions, and enjoy music and the beautiful surroundings since the 1870s. Chautauqua today is a summer resort colony, an educational institution, a center for the arts, and a community in its own right. Located on a lovely 700-acre site on the shores of Lake Chautauqua in southwestern New York State, much of the quiet charm of long ago is retained in the well-preserved Victorian architecture of the hotels and homes.

Two men of great vision, Mr. Lewis Miller and Mr. John H. Vincent, wanted to start a summer training center for the Methodist Episcopal Sunday school teachers in 1874, and selected Chautauqua as the ideal site. It became the first place in the United States to provide educational and religious studies during the summer vacation time, and to develop the concept of adult education. In 1904, the Tent Chautauqua Movement began as an independent spinoff of the New York colony and became a very popular way to bring entertainment to rural communities. It eventually faded out in 1932 with the advent of radio and automobiles, but the New York Chautauqua has continued to flourish and enrolls more then 2,000 students each summer in various programs.

Symphonic music was introduced to Chautauqua in 1909 when the New York Symphony appeared with Albert Stoessel as music director. When the New York Symphony merged with the New York Philharmonic in 1929, many of the former New York symphony musicians continued to come to Chautauqua each summer, and they formed the nucleus of what is now the Chautauqua Symphony Orchestra. Sergiu Comissiona became music director and principal conductor in 1976, and he continues the practice of engaging the finest guest artists available. Past seasons have welcomed conductors Arthur Fiedler, Robert Page, Skitch Henderson, Howard Hanson, Walter Hendl, and Julius Rudel; soloists Van Cliburn, Jessye Norman, Jerome Hines, Marilyn Horne, Yehudi Menuhin, Laszlo Varga, Susan Starr, Johanna Meier, Shirley Verrett, and many more. The Chautauqua Opera Association was inaugurated in 1929 and is also a vital ingredient of the summer program and presents six or seven operas each season.

The programming is varied and includes symphonic works, opera, chamber music, choral works, military bands, dance ensembles, jazz, folk groups, lectures, and dance concerts. In the early days, lectures and musical programs were held on a small, roofed platform with 2,000 backless benches. In 1893, a new amphitheater was built to accommodate 6,000 people and, though renovated, the same amphitheater is utilized today for symphony concerts and dance performances. For concerts requiring a more intimate setting, the 1,400 seat Norton Memorial Hall is used.

For tickets write to: Chautauqua Institution, Post Office Box 1095, Chautauqua, New York 14722. Telephone: (716) 357-5635.

For accommodations write: Chautauqua County Chamber of Commerce, 101 W. Fifth Street, Jamestown, New York 14701. Telephone: (716) 484-1101. For accommodation (listings only) write: Chautauqua Institution, Post Office Box 1095, Chautauqua, New York 14722. Telephone: (716) 357-5635.

FREE OUTDOOR PARK CONCERTS
New York City, New York
In August for three weeks

The Sheep Meadow, more than a half-mile long and covering over sixteen acres, may sound like an area in the high country of Colorado or New Mexico, when in fact, it is in Central Park in downtown Manhattan. Here is the site of the Free Outdoor Park Concerts, one of the most popular and best-attended festivals in the country. Modest estimates for attendance at a single concert have varied between 130,000 to 150,000 concertgoers! A crowd-pleaser is always the opening concert at Sheep Meadow with its special added attraction of a dramatic fireworks display at the end of the evening as the concluding bars of music are played!

In 1918, Adolph Lewisohn started the Stadium Concerts at the Lewisohn Stadium which he had donated to the City College of New York. These concerts established several outstanding precedents for out-of-season cultural events — the designation of a major symphony orchestra as the main ensemble (it has been the New York Philharmonic Symphony), and the launching of careers of relatively unknown artists . . . Marian Anderson, Eugene Ormandy, George Gershwin, and William Kapell. The stadium was razed in 1965, and then the New York Philharmonic Orchestra began its free concerts in various parks throughout the five boroughs of New York. The concerts have been jointly sponsored by the New York Philharmonic, the New York Department of Cultural Affairs, Herman Goldman Foundation, Jos. Schlitz Brewing Company, and were joined in 1976 by Exxon Corporation.

The programs include familiar classical orchestral works, as well as full orchestra presentations with instrumental soloists. Guest conductors have been Leonard Bernstein, Pierre Boulez,

Sarah Caldwell, Aldo Ceccato, André Kostelanetz, Erich Leinsdorf, Lorin Maazel, Eugene Ormandy, Thomas Schippers, and Zubin Mehta; and soloists Gina Bachauer, Stanley Drucker, Eileen Farrell, Garrick Ohlsson, Gerard Schwarz, and William Warfield. The programs are announced in advance in the New York newspapers and by public service announcements on television and radio. There are usually three concerts scheduled in each of the various parks. Most recently, the concert locations have been Van Cortlandt Park and the Botanical Garden in the Bronx; Clove Lake Park in Staten Island; Cunningham Park in Queens; Marine Park in Brooklyn; and Sheep Meadow in Central Park in Manhattan.

The Fourth of July during the Bicentennial year was a memorable concert as the orchestra's laureate conductor, Leonard Bernstein, not only conducted, but was also piano soloist for an all-American program featuring the conductor's works as well as those of Copland, Schuman and Gershwin. And thus concert-goers heard the program which the orchestra had taken on tour throughout the United States and Europe that same year!

For information write to: Free Park Concerts, New York Philharmonic, Avery Fisher Hall, Broadway at 65th Street, New York, New York 10023. Telephone: (212) 580-8700—also check New York newspapers!

For accommodations write to: New York Convention and Visitors Bureau, 90 E. 42nd Street, New York City, New York 10017. Telephone: (212) 687-1300.

MAVERICK SUNDAY CONCERTS
Woodstock, New York
July and August on Sunday afternoons

Woodstock brings to mind rock festivals, jazz concerts, summer theater, exhibits, and a retreat and colony for writers and artists, but here in the scenic hills of the Catskill Mountains of New York State are also the famous Maverick Sunday Concerts, "the oldest continuous chamber music series in the nation." At the turn of the century, Hervey White, novelist, poet, and architect, purchased land outside of Woodstock and named it "Maverick." Remembering a wild stallion from his boyhood days in Kansas, he had told his sister that "if I ever get a place of my own, I will call it 'The Maverick,' and it will be like a maverick belonging to no one, but also to whoever can get it!"

With the help of local young people, he built what he called his "music chapel" on the farmland and organized a Sunday concert series. The admission for the concerts was twenty-five cents, and in 1916 Mr. White announced that "these concerts will be devoted to that highest class of all music, known as chamber music, and will be given by a small group of musicians especially selected for that purpose. Let it be distinctly understood that while these will be social as well as artistic, they will not, in any way, seem objectionable to those of strict Sunday observance . . ." In those early days, the regular season for professional orchestral musicians ran but thirty-two weeks, and artists had time for an entire summer at Woodstock. These musicians had little chance to play chamber music during their regular concert series, so they relished getting together with other professional musicians to play chamber music.

Today, as in the earlier days, the charm of these Maverick Sunday Concerts lies in the opportunity to hear accomplished artists perform music in a wooded, rustic, and natural setting. The concert hall, nestled in a dense forest, is an unusual structure made of oak, pine, and chestnut, cut and milled locally. It has fifty-six paned windows in the front gable, and the roof along one side forms a huge porch. The hall has outstanding acoustical qualities, and seats 400 patrons with an additional area outside for listeners.

The programming, although primarily chamber music, spans the spectrum from traditional combinations of quintets, quartets, trios, and duos to the very latest contemporary music. In the past, there were performances of commissioned works of Henry Cowell, noted American composer, and Alexander Semmler, composer and music director of the Maverick Concerts from 1954 to 1969. Guest ensembles and artists engaged for past seasons have been the Tokyo String Quartet, The Concord String Quartet, Dorian Woodwind Quintet, The Philidor Trio, the Beaux Arts Quartet, Hoffman Trio, New York Chamber Soloists, and the Eastern Brass Quintet, and soloists Grant Johannesen, Walter Trampler, Lorin Hollander, William Kroll, Zara Nelsova, Ani Kavafian, Susan Davenny Wyner, Yehudi Wyner, and Jaime Laredo.

For tickets write to: Maverick Concerts, Inc., Post Office Box 102, Woodstock, New York 12498. Telephone: (914) 679-8746.

For accommodations write to: Woodstock Chamber of Commerce, Woodstock, New York 12498. Telephone: (914) 679-6234.

MOSTLY MOZART FESTIVAL
New York City, New York
Mid-July to the last week in August for six weeks

The Mostly Mozart Festival makes for mirth and merriment in music-making. One of New York City's major and most enjoyable summer musical events is this festival held in late July for six weeks. The music of Mozart is emphasized with a little Bach, Beethoven, Handel, Haydn, and Schubert as well. The concert series began in 1966 with William W. Lockwood, Jr., as festival director, and through the years all admission tickets have been offered at one popular price with special discounts for the purchase of ten tickets. The programs offer orchestra and choral works performed by the resident thirty-five-piece Festival Orchestra, on Monday, Wednesday, Friday, and Saturday evenings, and chamber music and recitals on Tuesday and Thursday evenings.

The festival abounds with new talent, both in quality and quantity, each season. A concertgoer is often in for a surprise when he hears an artist, known for his expertise as an instrumental soloist, "double in brass" by conducting. Some of the instrumental soloists who have made their conducting debut have been organists Anthony Newman and Karl Richter; pianists Christoph Eschenbach and Philippe Entremont; flutist Jean-Pierre Rampal; and violinist Pinchas Zukerman. A large number of artists have made their New York conducting debut at the festival (often, during a season, audiences are treated to ten different conductors for ten concerts!). Mario Bernardi, Maurice Abravanel, Sergiu Comissiona, Boris Goldovsky, Raymond Leppard, Eduardo Mata, Jorge Mester, Neville Marriner, Gerhard Samuel, Alexander Schneider, and Michael Tilson Thomas are a few of these performers. The concerts feature new artists, as well as those from the front ranks of the musical world. In recent seasons these have included: Emanuel Ax, Donald Gramm, Eugene Istomin, Byron Janis, Lili Kraus, Alicia de Larrocha, Jaime Laredo, Jessye Norman, Gerard Schwarz, Peter Serkin, Richard Stoltzman, and Benita Valente. Some of the many fine ensembles have been the Beaux Arts Trio, Boston Symphony Chamber Players, Cleveland Quartet, the Chamber Music Society of Lincoln Center, Guarneri Quartet, Alexander Schneider and Friends, and TASHI. All concerts are held in the 2,836-seat air conditioned Avery Fisher Hall at Lincoln Center at 8 P.M. with an addition bonus of a "pre-

concert" at 7 P.M. which presents many of the evening's soloists in special recital programs.

The festival promises something for everyone and every taste, and "for thousands of people in New York, Mozart is becoming as much a part of summer as the Good Humor Man."

For information and tickets write to: Mostly Mozart Festival, Avery Fisher Hall, Lincoln Center for the Performing Arts, Inc., 1865 Broadway, New York City, New York 10023. Telephone: (212) 874-2424.

For accommodations write to: New York Convention and Visitors Bureau, 90 E. 42nd Street, New York, New York 10017. Telephone: (212) 687-1300.

NAUMBURG ORCHESTRAL CONCERTS
New York City, New York
Four concerts scheduled between Memorial Day and Labor Day

The Central Park of 1905 was truly a pastoral setting with a ram or two, a flock of sheep, and a sheepherder. That same year, Elkan Naumburg decided that the park would be an ideal site to present free concerts for New York's citizens. He sponsored a symphony orchestra, and the concerts were held in an octagonal, pagoda-shaped bandstand with the audience sitting around the stand. In 1923, he donated another gift to the city: a new bandstand; and concerts have been staged continuously in the Mall at Central Park ever since, with audience attendance in excess of 8,000. After Elkan Naumburg's death in 1924, his family continued the concerts.

For many years, the musical events were held on the evenings of three holidays—Memorial Day, Fourth of July, and Labor Day; later a fourth concert was added on the approximate date of Elkan Naumburg's death, July 31. In 1976 the schedule was changed to the Sunday afternoon before the holidays.

Programs include vocal and instrumental recitals, chamber and symphonic music, and light operas. One concert each summer presents the music of an American composer and an opera in concert form.

Some of the outstanding talent at the concerts has been Richard Burgin, Maurice Peress, Jacques Singer, and Richard Woitach, conductors; Sidney Harth, Jaime Laredo, Joseph Silverstein, Zvi Zeitlin, violinists; Lorne Munroe and Leslie Parnas, cellists; and McHenry Boatwright, Judith Raskin, Benita Valente, and William Warfield, vocalists. The Empire Brass Quintet has also made an important contribution to the series.

In recent years, "New York is a Summer Festival," has been that city's proud boast, designed to lure crowds of visitors to the "Big Apple," but since 1905, the Naumburg Concerts have provided a "Summer Festival" for the good burghers of New York, as well.

For information write to: Naumburg Orchestral Concerts, Inc., 175 West 93rd Street, New York, New York 10025. Telephone: (212) 666-4413.

For accommodations write to: New York Convention and Visitor's Bureau, 90 E. 42nd Street, New York City, New York 10017. Telephone: (212) 687-1300.

SARATOGA PERFORMING ARTS CENTER
Saratoga Springs, New York
First week in July to the end of August for eight weeks

Saratoga Performing Arts Center aims to please, and it does! A few years ago when Maestro Eugene Ormandy, music director, was conducting at Saratoga, he mentioned that a nearby waterfall was so loud that the quieter passages in the music could not be heard. Anxious to correct the situation, the directors at Saratoga went to considerable expense and modified the flow of water! SPAC, as Saratoga Performing Arts Center is called, goes out of its way to provide fine facilities for its patrons. The Center, within the 1,500-acre Saratoga Springs State Park, has handsome and spacious landscaped grounds where patrons are able to stroll, relax, picnic, and attend concerts. Since its opening in 1966, SPAC has become one of the most important permanent summer festivals in New York and one of the most exciting in the country.

Keystones of the center are the Philadelphia Symphony Orchestra and the New York City Ballet, both of whom make their summer home at Saratoga. The first half of the season is devoted to ballet performances under the direction of Lincoln Kirstein, and the latter half to symphonic concerts with the Philadelphia Symphony Orchestra under the direction of Eugene Ormandy.

Other programming includes the in-residence Acting Company under the direction of John Houseman which offers outstanding theater productions. The ballet and orchestra perform Tuesday through Saturday evenings and the remaining evenings are reserved for chamber music concerts or entertainment by jazz or popular artists. Pre- and post-season activities also feature famous jazz performers and popular entertainment. Performances are held in the attractive and modern amphitheater providing 5,100 seats for patrons under cover and additional lawn seating for 10,000 concertgoers. The amphitheater acoustics are excellent, and the sweeping architectural design creates an illusion of an enclosed concert hall, although it is open at the back, making listening easy and enjoyable for the lawn patrons.

Guest artists and conductors who have appeared with the Philadelphia Symphony Orchestra are the best in their fields, for example: conductors Sarah Caldwell, Aaron Copland, Arthur Fiedler, Riccardo Muti, Charles Munch, Seiji Ozawa, John

Pritchard, Gunther Schuller, Leonard Slatkin, and Edo de Waart; pianists John Browning, Gina Bachauer, Byron Janis, Horacio Guiterrez, Garrick Ohlsson, and André Watts; vocalists Montserrat Caballé, Placido Domingo, Mignon Dunn, Ezio Flagello, Seth McCoy, Thomas Paul, Benita Valente, and Ruth Welting. SPAC also is proud of its "firsts"—the world premiere of Gian-Carlo Menotti's Symphony no. 1 in 1976, and Norman Dello Joio's "Songs of Remembrances" in 1977. "SPAC Specials" have included popular headliners as well: Pat Boone, Harry Chapin, Judy Collins, Oscar Peterson, Linda Ronstadt, Frank Sinatra, Earl Scruggs Revue, and Elton John.

Once known as "America's Greatest Spa," Saratoga Springs was a haven for those seeking mineral baths, health pavilions, and the finest in thoroughbred racing. Today Saratoga Springs is back in the running and winning—not only with horse racing, but with recreation, relaxation, and the best of the arts available.

For tickets write to: Saratoga Performing Arts Center, Saratoga Springs, New York 12866. Telephone: (518) 587-3330.

For accommodations write to: Saratoga Springs Chamber of Commerce, 297 Broadway, Saratoga Springs, New York 12866. Telephone: (518) 584-3255.

SPRING MUSIC FESTIVAL
Potsdam, New York
Last week in April for two days

The musical offerings at the Spring Music Festival last only two days, but they attain a high level of quality and interest. Miss Helen M. Hosmer, founder of the Crane Chorus and Orchestra in 1931, and later its director, was responsible for developing the Spring Music Festival. As the musical event grew in stature and reputation, it inspired the commissioning of major compositions for chorus and orchestra, and many well-known composers, soloists, and conductors were invited performers. Some of the conductors of international reputation have been Nadia Boulanger, Stanley Chapple, Lukas Foss, Howard Hanson, Thor Johnson, Robert Shaw, Michael Tilson Thomas, Virgil Thomson, Norman Dello Joio, and Sarah Caldwell.

Today, the Crane Chorus and Symphony Orchestra are still the main performing ensembles with guest conductors. During the 1978 season, in celebration of the forty-seventh annual festival, Aaron Copland conducted his own works for chorus, orchestra, and solo voice.

The performances are given on Saturday evenings and Sunday afternoons in the 1400-seat Helen M. Hosmer Concert Hall on the campus of State University College in Potsdam. Miss Hosmer was in attendance in 1976 at the opening of the hall named in her honor. There was a grand tribute given to this illustrious lady whose career has contributed much to the development of choral music and music education in the United States.

For tickets and information write to: Spring Festival Box Office, Crane School of Music, State University College at Potsdam, Potsdam, New York 13676. Telephone: (315) 268-2973.

For accommodations write to: Postdam Chamber of Commerce, Post Office Box 717, Potsdam, New York 13676. Telephone: (315) 265-5440.

SUMMER OF MUSIC ON THE HUDSON
Tarrytown, New York
*First week in July to the second week in August
for seven Saturday evenings*

One of the most beautiful and alluring places on the Hudson River is Tarrytown, New York, for there stands Lyndhurst, "one of the greatest houses in America." The mansion and grounds covering sixty acres have been maintained by the National Trust for Historic Preservation since 1964, and are the site of a music festival, Summer of Music on the Hudson. The great house was built in 1836 in Gothic Revival style by General William Paulding, an early mayor of New York City. It was called Knoll, Paulding's Villa, and in jest, Paulding's Folly. Later, a merchant named George Merritt bought it, renamed the estate Lyndhurst, beautified the grounds, and constructed an enormous greenhouse. Jay Gould became the next owner in 1880, adding his own touches and decorating the estate with Gothic-style furnishings. One of Mr. Gould's relatives left Lyndhurst to the National Trust, and now the mansion and the grounds are open for the public to enjoy.

Summer of Music on the Hudson concerts are held on Saturday evenings, and families are encouraged to come early, picnic, and enjoy the beautifully manicured gardens and grounds. The atmosphere is relaxed and informal — reminiscent of a small-town Sunday band-concert gathering. The programming is varied with music of composers from J.S. Bach to Walter Piston, and at the end of the season, there is one evening of popular music. The concerts usually employ full orchestra along with a guest vocalist or instrumentalist.

The County Symphony is the in-residence ensemble and is made up of the finest professional musicians who either live or work in Westchester County, New York. Music director, Stephen Simon, has conducted the orchestra since its first season in 1970, and during the winter season, he is music director of the Handel Festival at Kennedy Center in Washington, D.C. Guest artists are invited during the series and have included pianists Michel Block and Robert Goldsand; violinists Zina Schiff and Oscar Shumsky; vocalists Elinor Bergquist, Grayson Hirst, John Ostendorf, and Sofia Steffan.

The concerts are held on Saturday evenings near the great house in an area with a natural amphitheater and a beautiful vista of the Hudson River. A large yellow-and-white striped tent is available for those who wish to be under cover (and this permits concerts to be held rain or shine!). For those who wish to be under the stars, there is plenty of lawn space. As the mansion Lyndhurst is not open during concert hours, concertgoers may get a cursory look at the exterior—just enough to be tempted to return and see in detail this great house which represents the best of Hudson River Gothic.

For tickets and information write to: Summer of Music on the Hudson, c/o The County Symphony Association of Westchester, 635 South Broadway, Tarrytown, New York 10591. Telephone: (914) 631-0046.

For accommodations write to: Tarrytown Chamber of Commerce, South Broadway, Tarrytown, New York 10591. Telephone: (914) 631-1705.

SUMMERGARDEN
New York City, New York
Early June to early September for fourteen weekends

One of the world's most inviting and famous "parks" is the open air Abby Aldrich Rockefeller Sculpture Garden in the Museum of Modern Art in midtown Manhattan. From early June to early September, the Garden is open to the public, without charge, every Friday, Saturday, and Sunday evening from 6 P.M. to 10 P.M. to enjoy the sculpture and the beautiful surroundings. On Friday and Saturday evenings, free informal concerts are presented as well. In 1971, the Mobil Oil Corporation made a grant to the city which enables the Museum to open its Garden Gate at 8 West 54th Street for these very special and well-attended Summergarden series. The Garden is an urban oasis complete with many famous sculptures, splashing fountains, reflecting pools, and beds of flowers, shrubs, and trees. The large-scale sculpture collection is an art exhibition in its own right, displaying works of such masters as Calder, Maillol, Matisse, Moore, Oldenburg, Renoir, and Rodin. Those in attendance at the series may sit, relax, stroll, listen to the music, and enjoy the surroundings in a setting fit for the Muses!

The emphasis at the concerts is on young emerging artists and composers who are provided support and exposure to new audiences. The programming, innovative, and always interesting, is usually organized into four month-long series with jazz, Dixieland, country, blues, and ragtime in June; classical and contemporary works in July; unusual "new music" in August; and a combination of all in September. Dance and movement performances are also included in the season, and in 1978, a series called "Projects: Performance" featured performance art.

Many young songwriters and composers have had their works performed and premiered at Summergarden. Some of the most recent have been John and Carrie Carney, Michael Cohen, John Guth, Garrett List, Joan La Barbara, Charles Morrow, Tom McLaughlin, Suni Paz, Carl Rosenstock, Marga Richter, Cecil Taylor, John Watts, and Peter Zumo. The list of soloists and ensembles is lengthy, and some of these talented performers are guitarist William Matthews; pianists Julie Holtzman, David Morgan, Dwight Peltzer, and Vivian Taylor; and ensembles Ecstasy, Artie Miller's No Gap Generation Jazz Band, Newband, Wall Street Dixieland Band, L'Arema Chamber Ensemble, Small Planet, and the Ambrosian Chamber Ensemble.

There have been many fascinating evenings at the Summergarden series. One such was in 1976 when Kirk Nurock's Natural Sound Workshop premiered a work entitled, *Track,* a musical composition on how movement effects sound. "Two men started singing and jogging towards each other, until they collided, chest to chest, causing the sound to change. Then a group of five, clustered together both physically and sonically, crossed the room slowly, shaking their heads vigorously to shake the sound." The same year, a series called, "Hit Tunes From Flop

Shows" or "75 Years of the Great Music From Broadway's Biggest Turkeys" was presented. The audience (which usually averages 1,800 to 2,000, and had broken all attendance records to date) was told to guess the name of the show, and as a result, there was great interaction between audience and cast. The following year, concertgoers heard the premiere of two exciting works, both entitled *Wave Music,* by Charlie Morrow and Richard Hayman, which were played by forty unamplified celli.

Summergarden presents an exciting and interesting blend of the established masterworks in sculpture, along with the new, young, and sometimes experimental, presentations of music and dance!

For information write to: Summergarden, The Museum of Modern Art, 11 West 53rd Street, New York, New York 10019. Telephone: (212) 956-7298.

For accommodations write to: New York Convention and Visitors Bureau, 90 E. 42nd Street, New York City, New York 10017. Telephone: (212) 687-1300.

BREVARD MUSIC CENTER
Brevard, North Carolina
Last week in June to the second week in August for seven weeks

"The Summer Cultural Center of the South" is the proud claim of the Brevard Music Center. Nestled in the Smoky Mountains and the Pisgah National Forest in Transylvania County, thirty miles south of Asheville, is the little North Carolina community of Brevard. Most of the year, the rural town is quiet and serene, but Brevard begins bustling in June when over 300 students and 125 faculty come to the Brevard Music Center. Dr. James Christian Pfohl established a boys' summer music camp at Davidson College in 1936, and after World War II, the present site in Brevard was selected, and the Brevard Music Center came into existence.

The Center sponsors the Brevard Music Festival, the Translvania Music Camp, and at least eight other major performing organizations. The main thrust of the Center is on education and performance by young students who are enrolled in an intensive seven-week course, but much emphasis is placed on the festival performances, as well. There are over forty-five different programs offered during the season ranging from symphonic and chamber works to opera, light opera, choral works, and solo recitals. The Brevard Music Center Orchestra, the principal performing ensemble, is composed of instrumental artists-faculty and of advanced students from the Center. Dr. Henry Janiec has been artistic director of the Center since 1964, and in that capacity served as principal conductor of the orchestra and the opera workshop. Dr. Janiec says, "Brevard's 'Vacation with a Purpose' has become more than a slogan—it is a way of life for students, and a turning point in many important careers."

A new composer-in-residence program was initiated in 1978 with Elie Siegmeister as the Center's first guest to begin the "Chair-in-Composition" program. Audiences had the opportunity of hearing the composer's own compositions, some of which were premieres, and students have the opportunity to receive instruction. To augment an already high caliber of musical activity, a few guest artists are invited each year. Recent seasons have presented conductors Jamie Hafner, Emil Raab, Robert Shaw, and Ward Woodbury; vocalists Enrico di Giuseppe, Mary Costa, Jerome Hines, Marilyn Horne, James McCracken, Anna Moffo, Nell Rankin, Lorna Myers, and William Warfield; instrumentalists James Ceasar, Steven De Groote, Hans Richter-Haaser, Eugene List, Van Cliburn, Leonard Pennario, and Jerzy Kosmala.

Performances are held every Friday, Saturday, and Sunday evening in the Whittington-Pfohl Auditorium which seats 1,650 concertgoers. Monday through Wednesday evening concerts feature student performances utilizing the Concert Band, Transylvania Youth Orchestra, student recitals, and the Wind Ensemble. These concerts are usually held in the Straus Auditorium.

For tickets and information write to: Brevard Music Center, Post Office Box 592, Brevard, North Carolina 28712. Telephone: (704) 884-2011.

For accommodations write to: Brevard Chamber of Commerce, 35 W. Main Street, Brevard, North Carolina 28712. Telephone: (704) 883-3700.

EASTERN MUSIC FESTIVAL
Greensboro, North Carolina
Last week in June to the first week in August for six weeks

LISTEN, which stands for "Let it Sound To Everyone Near" is a program initiated by the Eastern Music Festival. LISTEN takes live performances of symphonic and chamber music to prisons, day care centers, housing projects, parks, homes for the aged, and camps; that is, to people who normally do not have a chance to hear classical music. LISTEN is one of many involvements of the Eastern Music Festival, the largest and most professional classical music festival in the South. It also has an intensive six-week institute of music studies, and a varied and interesting music festival.

Started as a small local music camp in 1962, the festival's music institute enrolls over 200 students and has a faculty of 85 teacher-performers. Sheldon Morgenstern, the festival's music director since its first season, feels that the kind of curriculum provided the students is unique: sectional rehearsals, sight-reading, master classes, theory and composition classes, and in turn, the students give concerts during the season. During the festival, audiences are offered over forty different orchestral and chamber music concerts performed by three different symphonic orchestras: the Eastern Philharmonic Orchestra composed of professional musicians from major symphonic orchestras in the country, the Eastern Symphony and Guilford Symphony Orchestra composed of students at the institute. The artists-in-residence program invites accomplished guest artists on a weekly basis to give master classes to students, and to perform as soloists with the Eastern Philharmonic Orchestra. Some of the resident faculty have been Richard Harrison, Robert Hause, Robert Helmacy, Bernice Maskin, Eugene Pridonoff, Carl Roskott, and Howard Weiss. Guest artists-in-residence in recent years have included Robert Bloom, James Buswell, Boris Brott, Leon Fleisher, Lillian Fuchs, Eugene Istomin, Veronica Jochum, Jaime Laredo, Yo-Yo Ma, Leonard Pennario, Walter Trampler, Beverly Wolff, and Zvi Zeitlin. Concerts are held on the campus of Guilford College, the oldest coeducational institution in the South, in the 1200-seat Dana Auditorium and the 800-seat Sternberger Auditorium.

Patrons, critics, and artists alike in 1978 enjoyed an American premiere of *Place Settings,* a work by Canadian composer, Louis Applebaum, which is a clever and provocative theater piece. It is a variation of a musical trick employed by Haydn in his *"Farewell Symphony"* when various players in the orchestra left individually; but in *Place Settings,* the players in the orchestra *appear* on stage to perform at staggered intervals!

Perhaps the best way to sum up Eastern Music Festival's activities is that the festival is growing better, not just older, every year!

For information write to: Eastern Music Festival, 712 Summit Avenue, Greensboro, North Carolina 27405. Telephone: (919) 272-2177.

For accommodations write to: Greensboro Chamber of Commerce, 217 North Greene Street, Greensboro, North Carolina 27402. Telephone: (919) 275-8675.

MORAVIAN MUSIC FESTIVAL AND SEMINAR
Winston-Salem, North Carolina
Mid-June for one week, every other year

The Moravians came from central Europe in the 1750s in search of a new home where they could enjoy religious freedom. Music permeated the whole fabric of Moravian life with songs and hymns for all occasions—harvesting, spinning, planting, traveling, marriages, and births. Music was their principal recreation; most Moravians could play an instrument and sing, and they would band together to play the music of Bach, Mozart, and Haydn. There were many composers among them who wrote hymns, choir anthems, and solo and duet songs—all of which echoed their strong religious convictions.

Thor Johnson felt that this wealth of music deserved to be more widely appreciated and known. His father was a Moravian minister, born in Wisconsin, who had lived in Winston-Salem since childhood, receiving his musical training there and establishing close ties with the Winston-Salem Moravian community. In 1950, Dr. Johnson founded the Early American Moravian Music Festival with the hope of bringing Moravian music into the mainstream of American culture. Dr. Johnson was music director and conductor of the festival until his death in 1975. Since that time Karl Kroeger has been music director and each festival has had a guest conductor to lead the chorus and orchestra. The festival is presented every two or three years in a location with a strong tie to the Moravian Church in America. Festivals have been held in Bethlehem, Pennsylvania; in New York City at several churches, including the First Moravian Church; in De Pere, Wisconsin; Dover, Ohio; and Winston-Salem on the campus of Salem College. All festivals are organized under the auspices of the Moravian Music Foundation and are offered along with seminars, workshops, ensemble and solo recitals, rehearsals, and concerts.

The tone of the festival is religious, with programs including orchestral, chamber, and choral music drawn from the archives of the Moravian Church in America. The fundamental theme is the presentation of the first twentieth-century performances of works by such eighteenth and nineteenth-century composers as John Antes (1740-1811), Johann Christian Geisler (1729-1815), Christian Ignatius Latrobe (1758-1836), David Moritz Michael (1751-1827), and Johann Friedrich Peter (1746-1813). Occasionally works of well-known eighteenth-century European composers, as well as American and European contemporary composers, are presented.

The festival orchestra is composed of local professional musicians and the chorus is made up of local professional and amateur vocalists and festival registrants. In recent years the guest artists have been John Nelson, Jeffrey Reynolds, and Richard Schantz, conductors; Doralene Davis, Jerry Jennings, Kim Kostenbader, Kay Phillips, and Elizabeth Pruett, vocalists; Martha Schrempel, pianist; and the Peabody Brass Ensemble with Wayne C. Cameron, conductor.

Open to the public without charge, the Moravian Music Festivals have gone far toward achieving Dr. Johnson's goal of making Moravian music widely known as a significant American musical tradition.

For information write to: The Moravian Music Foundation, Inc., 20 Cascade Avenue, Drawer Z, Salem Station, Winston-Salem, North Carolina 27108. Telephone: (919) 725-0651.

For accommodations: Contact Moravian Music Foundation, Inc. to determine the community where the festival will be held.

BALDWIN-WALLACE BACH FESTIVAL
Berea, Ohio
Last week in May for two days

"Vocal music will be taught for one dollar extra per term," announced the *Berea Advertiser* in 1848, advising students at Baldwin Institute that music instruction was available. This marked the beginning of a tradition at the Institute, later to be called Baldwin-Wallace College, which has stressed the importance of music to the present day. Dr. Albert Riemenschneider, who became head of the Music Department at Baldwin-Wallace in 1899, was a gifted organist and devotee of the music of Johann Sebastian Bach. He and his wife, Selma, started the Bach Festival in 1932, establishing it as the second oldest Bach Festival in the country. The festival programs include every category of Bach's works, including some of his rarely heard music. The programming permits the rotation of Bach's four major choral works on a four-year cycle and an attempt has been made to return to the use of the original language in each of Bach's choral works. The music of other composers of Bach's era is also produced, as in 1978 when the 300th anniversary of Vivaldi's birth was celebrated in an all-Vivaldi program.

The festival is held on the campus of Baldwin-Wallace College in Berea, a community fourteen miles southwest of Cleveland, Ohio. The concerts are performed in the Fanny Nast Gamble Auditorium in the Kulas Musical Arts Building which seats 650. Before the concerts, the Festival Brass Choir opens the evening with a series of chorals from the Merner Pfeiffer Terrace or from the tower of a nearby building. It is indeed a dramatic beginning and a fitting statement for the music which follows.

Music director Dwight Oltman engages the Festival Orchestra, the Baldwin-Wallace College Choir with choral director Stuart Raleigh, and the Motet Choir for the concerts, as well as guest vocalists and instrumentalists. Artists who have performed at the festival in recent seasons include Phyllis Bryn-Julson, Lili Chookasian, Betty Allen, Michael Sells, Thomas Paul, Elizabeth Mannion, Charles Treger, William Herbert, and Thomas Harmon.

For tickets write to: Baldwin-Wallace College Conservatory, Bach Festival Office, Berea, Ohio 44017. Telephone: (216) 826-2375.

For accommodations write to: Greater Cleveland Chamber of Commerce, 690 Union Commerce Building, Cleveland, Ohio 44115. Telephone: (216) 621-3300.

BLOSSOM MUSIC CENTER
Cuyahoga Falls, Ohio
Third week in June to the second week in September for twelve weeks

Cleveland not only has a first-class symphony orchestra, one of the wealthiest art museums in the country, one of the first professional resident theater companies in the nation, a famous auto-aviation museum, but it may also proudly boast of having one of the most respected cultural facilities in the United States: the Blossom Music Center. The Music Arts Association in 1966 found a beautiful 800-acre parklike area midway between Akron and Cleveland and decided it would be an ideal location for a music center. One hundred acres were developed with care and in close harmony with the remaining acreage of natural wooded forest, adjacent to Cuyahoga Valley National Park. The facility, named in honor of one of its initial contributors and ardent supporters of the Cleveland Orchestra, the Dudley S. Blossom family, opened in 1968 and became the official summer residence of the Cleveland Symphony Orchestra. Appropriately, the opening concert coincided with the fiftieth anniversary of the founding of the Cleveland Orchestra, and George Szell conducted Beethoven's *Consecration of the House* and the *Ninth Symphony.*

The musical offerings at Blossom are varied and appeal to every age and interest: ballet, symphonic performances, soft-rock, jazz, rhythm and blues, folk performers, children's day, band concerts for senior citizens, art exhibits, and festival forums.

Lorin Maazel, who became music director in 1970, upon the death of George Szell, has shared the podium with many fine conductors among whom have been Daniel Barenboim, Leonard Bernstein, Aaron Copland, André Kostelanetz, André Previn, Gunther Schuller, and William Steinberg. Guest artists have included pianists John Browning, Philippe Entremont, and Ruth Laredo; violinists Daviel Majeske, Itzhak Perlman, and Isaac Stern; and vocalist Montserrat Caballé, Grace Bumbry, Phyllis Curtin, Marilyn Horne, Donald Gramm, Luciano Pavarotti, and Beverly Sills. The Festival Chorus is composed of members of the Cleveland Orchestra Chorus and the Choral-Vocal Institute of the Blossom Festival School. Contemporary artists are an important part of the festival and have included Carol Channing, Ray Charles, Duke Ellington, Barry Manilow, Dolly Parton, Linda Ronstadt, and many, many more.

A growing cultural phenomenon is the association of a music school with a festival; Blossom Music Center is no exception. The Blossom Festival School, located on the nearby Kent State University campus, provides gifted musicians from all over the country highly concentrated musical instruction by members of the Cleveland Symphony Orchestra, teachers at Kent State University, and guest artists.

The Blossom pavilion where the concerts are held has won many awards for its innovative architecture and technology. The dramatic modern pavilion is placed at the base of a natural bowl with a one-and-three-quarter-acre fan-shaped slanting roof, an enormous oak stage with an acoustical shell, and no interior supporting columns. The airiness and openness of the area, the unobstructed view, and the excellent acoustics combine

to create a magical listening experience for the audience. The Pavilion seats 4,640 under the roof and an additional 13,500 may sit comfortably on the lawn and enjoy the concert with a clear view of the stage.

It has been said that Cleveland has "the best location in the nation" since it is within 500 miles of half the population of the United States and Canada. Blossom's perfect combination of a beautiful site, excellent acoustics, and topnotch performers provides this audience and others from elsewhere in the United States and the world with fine festival entertainment.

For information write to: Blossom Music Center, 1145 West Steels Corners Road, Cuyahoga Falls, Ohio 44223. Cleveland telephone: (212) 861-5674. Akron telephone: (216) 929-3048.

For accommodations write to: Cleveland Chamber of Commerce, Union Commerce Building, Cleveland, Ohio 44115. Telephone: (216) 621-3300. Or Akron Regional Development Board, One Cascade Plaza, Akron, Ohio 44308. Telephone: (216) 376-5550.

CINCINNATI MAY FESTIVAL
Cincinnati, Ohio
Mid-May for two weeks on Friday and Saturday evenings

Saengerfests, a tradition that grew up around the grape harvests when local singing groups gathered for merry "singing, eating, speechmaking, and imbibing the juice of generous grape" (according to a newspaper report), were the forerunners of the May Festival. Choral music came to Cincinnati with the first European settlers, mostly British and Germans; therefore, it is not surprising that Cincinnati had been a festival town forty years before the first May Festival occurred. These singing societies soon joined the choruses from Cleveland, Louisville, Detroit, and Saint Louis, and in 1867, there were over two thousand singers in the chorus at the gatherings. Inspiration for the first May Festival in 1873 came from Maria Longworth Nichols, a patron of the arts in Cincinnati, and Theodore Thomas, an eminent musical figure of the day.

The festival focus is on major choral works and opera repertoires. It offers choral music that is seldom heard, along with the great masterpieces. Some of the works commissioned for the festival have included Werner Henze's *Moralities*, Gian-Carlo Menotti's *Death of the Bishop of Brindisi*, and Margaret Johnson Bosworth's *Queen City Suite*. The orchestra, formerly directed by James Levine, and now with James Conlon as its new music director, is composed of Cincinnati Symphony Orchestra members with guest conductors and artists. The May Festival Chorus is a collective of children and adults from colleges, universities, clubs, societies, and seminaries in the area with a basic ensemble numbering 200 singers. The chorus is really the heart of the festival and the alumni members of the chorus total tens of thousands. (In 1968, the chorus numbered over 1,000 singers.) Among the outstanding conductors and soloists who have appeared at the festival are conductors Leonard Bernstein, Josef Krips, Julius Rudel, and Robert Shaw; vocalists Montserrat Caballé, Eileen Farrell, Maureen Forrester, Donald Gramm, Richard Lewis, Sherrill Milnes, Judith Raskin, Richard Tucker, and many others.

The festival is held in the Music Hall built in 1878 and referred to as "Renaissance with a touch of Gothic." In 1972, the Hall underwent massive renovation and now is considered one of the most beautiful and functional opera and symphony halls in the world. The refurbished auditorium seats 3,602 and is second in size only to New York's Metropolitan Opera House. The May Festival is a permanent institution in the city, and Cincinnatians are proud of it and their great musical tradition.

For information write to: Cincinnati May Festival, Community Ticket Office, 642 Race Street, Cincinnati, Ohio 45202. Telephone: (513) 381-2661.

For accommodations write to: Cincinnati Convention and Visitors Bureau, 200 West Fifth Street, Cincinnati, Ohio 45210. Telephone: (513) 621-2142.

PETER BRITT MUSIC FESTIVAL
Jacksonville, Oregon
Early August for fourteen days

Jacksonville, Oregon and its Britt Gardens are a very special place! Swiss-born Peter Britt settled in Jacksonville in 1852 at the height of the gold strikes. He started a land claim, built a home, created lush gardens, and pursued his vocation of photographer and portrait painter. His photographs of Oregon during the mid-nineteenth century are an important permanent pictorial record and are on display in the museum in Jacksonville. Britt and his family bestowed a legacy on the community and the Britt Gardens are now a historical landmark. John Trudeau, who founded the Peter Britt Music Festival in 1963, had been inspired by his visits to Tanglewood in Massachusetts as a member of the Boston Symphony Orchestra. When he moved to Oregon in 1951, he became deeply involved in the musical scene in Oregon and spent time exploring the countryside. It was then he discovered that Britt Gardens had excellent natural acoustics, that the community of Jacksonville had historical charm, and that the name *Britt* aroused people's curiosity. In other words, he felt it was a perfect place for a music festival.

The festival presents symphonic works, chamber music, and recitals with vocal and instrumental soloists. The festival orchestra, numbering about fifty musicians is made up of members of the Portland Symphony Orchestra and other major symphony orchestras on the West Coast. The festival chorus, under the direction of Lynn Sjolund, consists of members of the Portland Symphony Choir and the Rogue Valley Chorale. Featured guest artists in recent years have been pianists William Doppmann, Robert Guralnik, Gerhard Puchelt, and Tomas

Svobada; violinists Christiane Edinger, Martin Friedman, conductor Stanley Chapple, and ensemble groups such as the Florestan Trio, Philadelphia String Quartet, and the German Singing Club. The programming is varied and includes both familiar and lesser-known works of the masters.

The evening orchestra concerts and the daytime youth concerts are held in an outdoor pavilion. This was completely renovated in 1978, and is of a modified contemporary design ideally suited to blend into the hillside setting of grassy slopes and native pine and madrona trees. Seating is virtually unlimited and patrons are advised to bring blankets and folding chairs. The afternoon indoor recitals are held in the historic United States Hotel ballroom in Jacksonville. Seating capacity is 200.

Jacksonville, designated a National Historical site, has many public buildings and homes which have been restored to their original condition, and many of these homes are open to the public. Nearby is Ashland, home of the famous Oregon Shakespeare Festival. Performances of the highest caliber are given daily, and visitors may tour the three special theater facilities and the small, but interesting, Shakespeare Museum. Scenic wonders and beauty abound in the Rogue River area, and for the adventuresome, river trips offer a fascinating diversion.

For ticket information write to: Peter Britt Gardens Music and Arts Festival, Post Office Box 669, Jacksonville, Oregon 97530. Telephone: (503) 899-1821.

For accommodations write to: Jacksonville Chamber of Commerce, 185 North Oregon Street, Jacksonville, Oregon 97530. Telephone: (503) 899-8118.

BETHLEHEM BACH FESTIVAL
Bethlehem, Pennsylvania
Mid-May for two weekends

Trombones from the belfry of the Moravian Church herald the opening of the Bethlehem Bach Festival. The custom began in 1900 with the first festival, and has continued each year. Tradition and continuity are clearly important to the festival and its singers, for out of a choir of 200, twelve have sung with the choir for over forty years! In the 1880s Bethlehem, the site of the festival, was a small Moravian village with a large German Protestant population. They were steeped in a strong musical heritage from Europe and were keenly interested in choral music. Among them was Dr. J. Fred Wolle, inheritor of these musical traditions, who travelled in Munich in 1884 and studied with Joseph Rheinberger, a famous conductor, organist, and devotee of Bach. Inspired by his studies, Dr. Wolle returned to Bethlehem and resolved to devote his life to making Bach's music known. "By sheer determination, bullying, and cajoling," he was able to convince the choir to sing the music of his favorite composer, and he founded the Bach Choir in 1898. Two years later, the first complete American performance of Bach's Mass in B Minor was performed.

Since the first festival in 1898, there have been only four musical directors. Dr. Ifor Jones, music director from 1939 to 1969 is credited with presenting over 140 Bach cantatas, 30 of which were sung for the first time in the United States! Upon his retirement, Dr. Alfred Mann took over as director and continues the custom of presenting choral and instrumental works of Johann Sebastian Bach, as well as the Mass in B Minor each season. The 1972 festival was an important celebration under his reign, as it marked the choir's 100th performance of the Mass!

The all-volunteer choir is composed of local singers of diverse backgrounds—housewives, businessmen, mill workers, farmers, students, and teachers — who rehearse throughout the year for the festival performances. Guest soloists of international reputation are engaged and have included Helen Boatwright, Kathryn Bouleyn, Charles Bressler, Phyllis Bryn-Julson, Lois Marshall, Seth McCoy, and Thomas Paul. Concerts are held on the beautiful hillside campus of Lehigh University in the Packer Memorial Chapel. The chapel seats 1100, but when the weather is pleasant, additional seating is available on the lawn outside. The choir has toured throughout the United States and met with great acclaim, but perhaps its most memorable journey was in 1976 when the entire choir and orchestra travelled to Germany to sing in Bach's own church in Leipzig.

For ticket information write to: The Bach Choir of Bethlehem, Main and Church, Streets, Bethlehem, Pennyslvania 18018. Telephone: (215) 866-4382.

For accommodations write to: Bethlehem Chamber of Commerce, 11 West Market Street, Bethlehem, Pennsylvania 18018. Telephone: (215) 867-3788.

ROBIN HOOD DELL CONCERTS
Philadelphia, Pennsylvania
Mid-June to the last week in July for seven weeks

World-class musical performances for the price of a newspaper? Where, but at the famed Robin Hood Dell Concerts in Philadelphia! The tickets are free, and obtained from coupons which appear in the daily Philadelphia newspaper. The policy of free general admission dates from the first concert in 1930 when a grant was provided by the City of Philadelphia, and this tradition has continued ever since. Scheduling world-renowned conductors and soloists is the hallmark of the festival. The Philadelphia Symphony Orchestra is in summer residence during the festival and the musical director is Eugene Ormandy, who shares the podium with some of the great names in the conducting world: Franz Allers, Leonard Bernstein, Daniel Barenboim, André Kostelanetz, James Levine, Zubin Mehta, Mstislav Rostropovich, Klaus Tennstedt, and Edo de Waart. The concerts' musical fare is usually symphonic works (occasionally light classics or musicals are performed) and a full orchestra with solo vocalists or instrumentalists is normally used. The soloists, engaged from the international circuit have included such stars as singers Regine Crespin, Mignon Dunn, Robert Merrill, Roberta Peters, Leona Mitchell, Paul Plishka, Florence Quivar, Rita Shane, and Beverly Sills; pianists Gina Bachauer, Jorge Bolet, Jerome Lowenthal, André Watts, Van Cliburn, and José Iturbi; violinists Yehudi Menuhin, William de Pasquale, Henryk Szeryng, and Isaac Stern.

Performances are held three times a week in the new Robin Hood Dell West facility which opened in 1976 at Fairmount Park, west of downtown Philadelphia. It is said that someone viewing the original Robin Hood Dell for the first time noted the similarity to Sherwood Forest, and thus it was named! There are 5,000 reserved seats under cover in the outdoor pavilion and an additional 10,000 general admission seats on benches and on the lawn, under the stars. The newspaper coupons mailed to the Recreation Department to obtain tickets are for these general admission seats.

For information write to: Robin Hood Dell Concerts, Inc., 1617 John F. Kennedy Blvd., Philadelphia, Pennsylvania 19103. Telephone (215) 567-0707.

For accommodations write to: Philadelphia Convention and Visitor's

Bureau, 1525 John F. Kennedy Blvd., Philadelphia, Pennsylvania 19102. Telephone: (215) 864-1976.

TEMPLE UNIVERSITY MUSIC FESTIVAL
Ambler, Pennsylvania
First week in July to the last week in August
for nine weeks

There is lots of good music as well as history in the Valley Forge country of Pennsylvania. For the history buff there's Valley Forge Park, Brandywine Battlefield and Museum, Bowman's Hill Observation Tower, Washington Crossing State Park, the Old Ferry Inn and New Hope. For the music enthusiasts, there's the Temple University Music Festival offering a wide variety of musical entertainment each summer. The festival was inaugurated in 1968 under the inspiration and guidance of President Millard E. Gladfelter, then president of Temple University, and Dr. David Stone, dean of the College of Music at Temple. They wanted a summer musical event at the university to benefit both the students and the community-at-large. The first seven years, the festival functioned as a festival-institute organized in the fashion of Aspen or Tanglewood, but in 1975, the Institute was eliminated and since that time, emphasis has been on the presentation of public concerts.

The festival scheduling offers a variety of events every day of the nine-week season which include symphonic concerts with guest conductors, vocalists and instrumentalists, ballet troupes, dance ensembles, opera, jazz and pop soloists, and groups. The prestigious Pittsburgh Symphony Orchestra is in residence at the festival with Sergiu Comissiona as artistic director and André Previn as music director. These conductors have shared the podium in recent years with such renowned artists as James Conlon, Aaron Copland, Henry Mancini, Eduardo Mata, John Nelson, Julius Rudel, and Leonard Slatkin. Outstanding guests in both the popular and classic fields of entertainment have appeared including vocalists, Martina Arroyo, Tony Bennett, Johnny Cash, Ella Fitzgerald, Theresa Kubiak, Gordon MacRae, Helen Reddy, Jess Thomas, and Benita Valente; and instrumentalists, John Browning, Eugene Istomin, Lorin Hollander, Mark Kaplan, Paul Badura-Skoda, Yo-Yo Ma, Rosalyn Tureck, Ruggiero Ricci, and André Watts. Ensemble groups have included the Bach Aria Group, Benny Goodman Sextet, Kingston

Trio, Earl Scruggs Review, Preservation Hall Jazz Band, and the Woody Herman Orchestra.

The concerts are held in the 3000-seat Festival Hall adjacent to the University on the suburban Ambler campus, fifteen miles north of Philadelphia. The grounds around the hall are beautifully landscaped and include a sculpture garden open to the public for pre- and post-concert strolling.

The Temple University Music Festival claims, "You can get here, from there!". . . and once you're there, you are indeed treated to a star-filled evening.

For information write to: Temple Music Festival, Temple University, Philadelphia, Pennsylvania 19122. Telephone: (215) 787-8318.

For accommodations write to: Philadelphia Convention and Visitors Bureau, 1525 J.F. Kennedy Blvd., Philadelphia, Pennsylvania 19102. Telephone: (215) 864-1976.

NEWPORT MUSIC FESTIVAL
Newport, Rhode Island
Mid-July for ten to fourteen days

Newport's Bellevue Avenue is *The Great Gatsby* revisited, for here in the late nineteenth century, the Astors, Belmonts, Berwinds, Vanderbilts, and other affluent financiers and industrialists built their summer "cottages," which in fact, are palatial, grandiose summer mansions with beautifully landscaped grounds. Newport is still the center of much activity in the summer—sailing regattas, tennis matches, and a mecca for sun bathers. History and architecture buffs may visit many interesting eighteenth, nineteenth, and twentieth-century public buildings and homes; and music enthusiasts may attend the Newport Music Festival. The hallmark and "plus" of the festival are the interesting programs performed by fine talent in a unique and elegant setting, since many of the concerts are presented in these lavish old mansions.

In 1968, Glen Sauls, founder of the Metropolitan Opera Studio, started the Romantic Music Festival in Newport with the Newport Preservation Society as co-sponsor for the event. Concerts were held in the ballrooms, music rooms, and salons of these beautiful homes, and they emphasized almost exclusively the forgotten romantic music of the nineteenth and twentieth centuries. In 1976 when Mark P. Malkovich III became general director, he expanded the programming to include not only relatively unknown nineteenth-century works, but also the familiar classics. He presents premieres each year as he feels that the "Newport Music Festival attracts a very sophisticated, select audience who has come to expect premieres, the unusual; music they can't get elsewhere."

The programs include chamber music, song recitals, mixed vocal and instrumental music, ballet, and a film series. There are usually three concerts a day: one in the morning, one in the late afternoon, and one in the evening. The artists, many of whom are repeats from past seasons, have included pianists Peter Basquin, Jean-Philippe Collard (who made his United States debut in Newport in 1977), Peter Frankl, Agustin Anievas, and Raymond Lewenthal; violinists James Buswell and Erick Fried-man; vocalists Glorietta Allison, Regine Crespin, John Aler, In-Soo Park, and Rose Wildes; cellist Leshek Zavistovski and Jeffrey Solow. Dance ensembles have included soloists from the Royal Danish Ballet, Erick Hawkins Dance Company, and the Mariano Parra Spanish Dance Theatre.

Some of the concert sites are Elms, built in 1901 and fashioned after a French chateau; Rosecliff, built in 1902 in a style reminiscent of Le Grand Trianon at Versailles; Chateau Sur-Mer, a lavish Victorian-style estate built in 1852, and Hammer-smith Farm, a summer White House between 1961 and 1963. Of particular note is the mansion Breakers, one of the most imposing and spectacular of all. Built in 1895 by Cornelius Vanderbilt, it resembles a sixteenth-century north Italian palace. Concerts are often given in the Great Hallway seating 400. Marble House, another sumptuous mansion was built in 1892 by William Vanderbilt. Two hundred concertgoers may enjoy per-formances in the Gold Ballroom surrounded by marble pillars, gold carved cherubs, crystal chandeliers, and Greek and Roman statuary. Ballet and larger ensemble presentations are held in Rogers High School Auditorium, the Church of the Patriots, and St. Joseph's Church.

Newport Music Festival is special with its all-encompassing ambience. It is a truly visual, social, and musical delight!

For tickets write to: Newport Music Festival, 50 Washington Square, Newport, Rhode Island 02840. Telephone: (401) 846-1133.

For accommodations write to: Newport County Chamber of Com-merce, 10 American Cup Avenue, Newport, Rhode Island, 02486. Telephone: (401) 847-1600.

SPOLETO FESTIVAL U.S.A.
Charleston, South Carolina
Last week in May to early June for two weeks

Spoleto, a small and picturesque hilltown north of Rome in Italy, has been the site of the world's most comprehensive arts festival since being founded by Gian Carlo Menotti in 1958. Maestro Menotti, the world-renowned composer, has been searching for eighteen years for a site for an American counterpart to his "Festival of Two Worlds" in Italy. In 1977, he selected Charleston, South Carolina. When Menotti was asked why he had chosen Charleston, he replied, "It would be easy to attribute my decision to the unique beauty of Charleston: the magic of its streets, the noble charm of the buildings, the warmth of its citizens; but that is not the real reason. . . . It is a unique and fertile ground for the young with new ideas and a dignified home for the masters. . . . It is a much-needed sign of hope in this age of suspicion and mistrust when two beautiful towns so different and so far away from each other, through the common quest for beauty, unfurl the flag of friendship."

Spoleto and Charleston do have similarities, though—an historical and aesthetic richness in their architecture and a strong musical heritage. Charleston, considered America's most beautifully preserved eighteenth-century city, had its first musical concerts in the mid-eighteenth century and many of the eighteenth and nineteenth-century homes, gardens, plantations, and churches have been lovingly preserved.

Spoleto Festival U.S.A. offers a season of total immersion in all the arts: symphonic and chamber music, opera, dance, ballet, jazz, visual arts, theater, and a film series. The festival's music director, Gian Carlo Menotti and artistic director, Christopher Keene, invite internationally-known artists, as well as young talented musicians, to the festival. The festival orchestra is composed of young musicians from universities and conservatories throughout the country. Some of the performers in past seasons have been vocalists Marvellee Cariaga, Patricia Craig, Ester Hinds, Johanna Meier, Magda Olivero, and Jack Trussel; conductors Joseph Flummerfelt, Christopher Keene, David Oren, and Clayton Westerman; dance and ballet ensembles: Ballets Felix Blaska, Eliot Feld Ballet, Dance Theatre of Harlem, and the Ohio Ballet. Chamber music concerts directed by Charles Wadsworth have included instrumentalists James Buswell, Anthony Newman, Yo-Yo Ma, Peter Serkin, Emanuel Ax, Ani Kavafian, and Richard Goode.

The festival events are scheduled daily and are presented in many historic and charming theaters, auditoriums, courtyards, gardens, parks, and plantations throughout the city. Some of these locations are the 463-seat Dock Street Theatre, built in 1736 and used for chamber music concerts, recitals, and theater productions; the 700-seat Garden Theatre; the 2700-seat Gaillard Municipal Auditorium, used for ballet, opera, dance and large symphony concerts; the outdoor Cistern of the College of Charleston, for ballet and symphonic concerts; Charles Towne Landing for jazz concerts; and many churches and plantations in and around Charleston. Mini-festivals are held in the parks during the daytime and offer mime, craft and puppet shows, instant theater, and small musical concerts.

Not long ago, Charleston was known as "America's Best Preserved Secret." Since Spoleto Festival U.S.A. arrived in town, with its cultural cloudburst of opera, music, theater, and dance, it stands in the first rank of American music festivals and has the recognition it deserves.

For information write to: Spoleto Festival U.S.A., P.O. Box 704, Charleston, South Carolina 29402. Telephone: (803) 722-2764.

For accommodations write to: Chamber of Commerce Tourist Information Center, Calhoun Street, Charleston, South Carolina 29402. Telephone: (803) 722-8338.

SEWANEE SUMMER MUSIC CENTER
Sewanee, Tennessee
Last week in June to the last week in July for five weeks

A fairly new phenomenon has caught on in the country: the summer music camps. And it has become a way of life for many aspiring music students. Some camps are located in rustic, rural areas, and others on school campuses. Sewanee is an attractive blend of both, as it is located in a quiet community midway between Chattanooga and Nashville on the campus of the University of the South. Situated on the Cumberland Plateau, the campus grounds have over 10,000 acres of mostly unspoiled woodland forests. The beautiful sandstone buildings on campus, covered with ivy, are reminiscent of Oxford in England. Roy Harris, noted American composer, brought music to the area in 1950 as conductor of the Cumberland Forest Festival. Seven years later, the Sewanee Summer Music Center was started

111

with thirty students with Julius Hegyi as conductor. Today the student body numbers 200.

The primary emphasis at the Center is on instrumental music with instruction being given in most musical instruments — piano, organ, strings, woodwind, brass, and percussion. A five-week course includes study in chamber music repertoire, orchestra training, harmony, sightreading, composition, conducting, and private study. As at Aspen and Tanglewood, the Center blends study with performances, for all students play in weekly chamber and orchestra concerts. There are three symphony orchestras at the Music Center; the Sewanee Symphony for advanced students; the Cumberland Orchestra for students with less previous experience; and the Sewanee Festival Orchestra composed of faculty, staff, and selected students. Faculty members are musicians from symphonic orchestras and conservatories all over the country and include pianists Martha Bartles, Elaine Harriss, and Julian Martin; violinists Aaron Kronsnick, Ann Spurbeck; Robert Strava, and Kishiko Suzumi; cellists Martha McCrory, director of the Center since 1963, and Peter Spurbeck. Guest conductors invited to the center in recent years have been Amerigo Marino, Richard Bales, Richard Burgin, Henri Temianka, Arthur Winograd, Hugh Wolff, and Kenneth Moore. Concerts are held on weekends in the 1,000-seat Guerry Hall at the University of the South. Chamber music is featured on Saturday afternoon, and symphony orchestra programs on Sunday afternoons.

For ticket information write to: Sewanee Summer Music Center, Sewanee, Tennessee 37375. Telephone: (615) 598-5931.

For accommodations write to: Chattanooga Chamber of Commerce, 819 Broad Street, Chattanooga, Tennessee 37402. Telephone: (615) 267-2121.

INTERNATIONAL FESTIVAL-INSTITUTE AT ROUND TOP
Round Top, Texas
Second week in June to the last week in July for six weeks

Texas is noted for "bigness," but the smallest incorporated city in Texas (population estimated at between forty-seven and ninety-two people) is the site of a significant classical music festival, Round Top. The community, Round Top, named for a house with a rounded roof, was a landmark for arriving stage coaches in days gone by. In the 1840s the area was settled by German and Czech immigrants—and their influence is felt today in their language, architecture—even in their cuisine (rumor has it that some Texas barbecues there are served with sauerkraut and spaetzle). James Dick, born in Kansas, and educated in Texas, New York, and London, founded the Festival-Institute in 1971, and chose the site because of its historical value, its cultural and ethnic heritage, and simply because he liked the Texas landscape. He felt that "Round Top was a cultural Switzerland, a neutral ground near urban centers . . . and it was rural, with real farmers and real people who also had an artistic tradition." An accomplished musician, the only pianist to win top prizes in 1966 in three competitions (Tchaikovsky, Leventritt, and Busoni), Mr. Dick is the driving force and inspiration behind all of the activities at Round Top. Described as "indefatigable educator, ubiquitous fund-raiser, imaginative impresario and career philospher," he has often been the featured pianist at the concerts.

The main emphasis at Round Top is on the six-week teaching institute whereby sixty students from all over the United States are offered advanced study in piano and strings, chamber music, and orchestra performances. They make up the forty-eight-member festival orchestra called the Texas Festival Chamber Orchestra with conductor, Leon Fleisher. Students are also offered seminars by noted musicologists and music critics. After the season, students travel to play some "philanthropic in-service" concerts in hospitals, nursing homes, and schools. The faculty, composed of internationally famed musicians, not only teaches at the Institute, but are featured soloists at the concerts. Some of these have been pianists Steven De Groote, Leonard Pennario, Patricia Zander; violinists Ida Kavafian, Young-Uck Kim, and Isidor Saslav, concertmaster; cellists Yo-Yo Ma and Yehuda Hanani.

Festival Hill, the name given to the gently rolling thirty-acre site in Round Top, is within two hours' driving time of Austin, Houston, and San Antonio. There are several unique facilities where the concerts are held: The Mary Moody Northern Pavilion, the world's largest transportable stage with space for a full orchestra and grand piano; the Dalies Frantz Chamber Music Court; and the William Lockhart Clayton Guest House, a restored 1870 Victorian farmhouse. Many concerts are held in the Sid W. Richardson Concert Square, an oak-shaded courtyard

surrounded by the big U-shaped farmhouse. It is not unusual to have katydids or scissortails singing from the cedar trees, competing with the musical offerings. Round Top is communing with the Muses, and if things continue to happen at Festival Hill, Round Top, it may soon become the "Tanglewood of Texas" or the "Marlboro of the South."

For tickets and information write to: The Festival-Institute at Round Top, Post Office Drawer 89, Round Top, Texas 78954. Telephone: (713) 249-3129.

For accommodations write to: San Antonio Chamber of Commerce, 602 E. Commerce Street, San Antonio, Texas 78296. Telephone: (512) 227-8181. Or Houston Chamber of Commerce, 1100 Milam Street, Houston, Texas 77002. Telephone: (713) 651-1313.

COMPOSERS' CONFERENCE
AND CHAMBER MUSIC CENTER
Johnson, Vermont
Last week in July for two weeks

"No matter how enervating one day might have been for the musicians, it was not unusual for an ensemble to gather after a concert to play yet another piece. In the late evening they would not play modern music, but rather something more traditional . . . like Mozart, to clear the ears!" That is how conference director, Mario Davidovsky, sums up the feeling of enthusiasm which prevails at the Composers' Conference. Each summer at Johnson State College in northern Vermont, fifteen or more students are involved in an intensive two-week study at the Composers' Conference. They are selected from over ten times as many applicants after careful screening of manuscripts which they submit. Upon acceptance students arrive with two compositions to be read, scrutinized, rehearsed, and performed by an outstanding staff of twenty-five or more professional musicians. Each year an established composer is asked to the conference to assist Mario Davidovsky and music director Efrain Guigui critique the young composers' work. Both directors feel that only here in all the United States can young composers hear their pieces played by a full symphonic orchestra with professional and amateur musicians, walk away with two tapes of their own compositions, and be in such close contact with renowned composers.

The conference was started in 1945 by Alan Carter, founder of the Vermont Symphony Orchestra. In those days, Carter felt that contemporary music was rarely performed, and less often understood, and he wanted young composers to have a chance for their work to be recognized and performed. Middlebury, Connecticut, was the original site of the festival, and shortly thereafter it moved to Bennington College, where it remained for twenty-five years. In 1974, the Composers' conference was moved to Johnson State College, a beautiful hilltop campus in the Green Mountains of northern Vermont, where it now has a permanent summer home.

Over the years, outstanding composers have been invited to the conference: Bulent Arel, Milton Babbitt, Donald Martino, Roger Sessions, and Richard Wernick. More recently to augment the already-successful Composers' Conference and the Chamber Music Center, also directed by Efrain Guigui, two workshops have been added — The Choral Institute with Iva Dee

Hiatt as director in 1976, and the Collegium of Early Music in 1977. All workshops offer amateurs, students, and professional musicians two weeks of exposure to baroque, classical and romantic music with seminars, coaching, lectures, rehearsals, and concerts.

The public is encouraged and cordially invited to attend the free concerts at the Dibden Auditorium, seating 500, which is on the Johnson State College campus. Composers' concerts are held on Wednesday, Friday, and Saturday evenings and the other workshop concerts at various times during the week. What better place to hear new music being born and to attend a performance where the "composers are the stars!"

For information write to: Composers' Conference and Chamber Music Center, Inc., Post Office Box 192, Hyde Park, Vermont 05655. Telephone: (802) 888-4325; during the conference: (802) 635-2356.

For accommodations write to: Lake Champlain Regional Chamber of Commerce, 131 Main Street, Burlington, Vermont 05401. Telephone: (802) 863-3489. Or St. Albans Chamber of Commerce, 128 Main Street, St. Albans, Vermont 05478. Telephone: (802) 524-2444.

MARLBORO MUSIC FESTIVAL
Marlboro, Vermont
July until mid-August for eight weekend concerts

The Marlboro Music Festival is certainly one of the most prestigious chamber music gatherings in the country. The festival joins together accomplished mature musicians with young professional musicians, not just for performances, but for the purpose of learning, exchanging ideas, and sharing musical experiences and knowledge.

The festival began in 1950 as the inspiration of music devotees Adolf and Herman Busch; Marcel, Louis and Blanche Moyse; and Rudolf Serkin, who banded together to start an informal summer music program. Soon it evolved into a very special gathering of the world's most distinguished artists who, since that time, have been producing a superior caliber of music. Rudolf Serkin, the eminent pianist, has directed the festival since 1951 and has upheld the festival's philosophy: "Everyone at Marlboro is a student . . . there are no teachers, no pupils, only participants. Everyone plays together on an equal basis, both giving and receiving musical experiences." Serkin makes good the philosophy, for just as everyone plays music together, they also work together. It has not been unusual to see Mr. Serkin sharing the dining room cleanup duties or lining up, plastic tray in hand, at the cafeteria!

The emphasis is strictly on chamber music performed by the participating musicians; there are no outside guest artists. The seventy-five musicians are concert artists, members of symphony orchestras, members of professional chamber ensembles, and gifted younger talent. During the eight-week season, they study and play a large repertoire combining brass, strings, voice, woodwind, and piano in varying combinations ranging from large ensembles to duos. Each week, in excess of one hundred works are studied and out of these, seven to nine are performed for the public on weekends. No advance notice is given as to the program or its performers as it is the outgrowth of works studied that particular week.

The festival has attracted many musical giants including Pablo Casals, Aaron Copland, Pina Carmirelli, Lukas Foss, Felix Galimir, Vladimir Horowitz, Eugene Istomin, Lilian Kallir, Jaime Laredo, James Levine, Leslie Parnas, Alexander Schneider, Isaac Stern, and Benita Valente.

Chamber music ensembles have been formed as a result of musicians working together at Marlboro; some of these have been the Guarneri, Cleveland, and the Vermeer String Quartets. Many members of the Chamber Music Society of Lincoln Center are alumni of Marlboro.

A contemporary composer's program was initiated at Marlboro in 1960 in cooperation with the Fromm Foundation and is under the direction of Leon Kirchner. Accomplished composers and young not-yet-established composers are invited to prepare their works to be performed by the participating musicians at the center. The list of composers is long and impressive: Elliott Carter, Aaron Copland, Samuel Barber, Lukas Foss, Walter Piston, Paul Chihara, Roger Sessions, Barbara Kolb, George Crumb, David Del Tredici, and many others. Marlboro is located in the verdant foothills of the Green Mountains in southern Vermont. The festival, held on the campus of picturesque Marlboro College, offers performances to the public on Friday and Saturday evenings and Sunday afternoons during the season. The concerts are given in Persons Auditorium, a handsome wooden structure resembling a sturdy Norse banquet hall, which has seating for only 650 concertgoers and is often sold out well in advance of the event. The entrance to the Marlboro Music Festival has a road sign reading, "Caution Musicians At Play." Where could this be more appropriate than in this Marlboro country?

For information write to: Before June 1: Marlboro Music Festival, 135 South 18th Street, Philadelphia, Pennsylvania 19103. After June 1: Marlboro Music Festival, Marlboro, Vermont 05344. Telephone: (802) 254-8163.

For accommodations: Chamber of Commerce, 180 Main Street, Brattleboro, Vermont 05301. Telephone: (802) 254-4565.

VERMONT MOZART FESTIVAL
Burlington, Vermont
Mid-July to the first week in August for three weeks

The Vermont Mozart Festival is really a moving experience. It does have a home base — Burlington, but it travels around the Lake Champlain resort area and other communities to give many Vermonters a chance to savor its fine musical fare.

The festival started in 1974 and was under the sponsorship of the University of Vermont for four years. In 1977, the University dropped its involvement and the Vermont Festival Association became the sponsor and retained noted oboist, Melvin Kaplan, as artistic director.

The festival's principal ensemble, the Vermont Mozart Festival Orchestra, composed of guest artists and professional musicians in the area, performs along with internationally-known guest soloists, instrumentalists, and ensembles. Programming includes the music of Mozart and other "durable" composers as well. Some of the guest artists in recent years have been Charles Bressler, tenor; Julius Baker and John Solum, flute; Menahem Pressler and Harriet Wingreen, piano; and James Chapman, director of the University of Vermont Choral Union. Ensembles have included the Beaux Arts Trio, Emerson String Quartet, New York Chamber Soloists, and the University of Vermont Choral Union. There are workshops and master classes given in conjunction with the festival, as well as a free lecture series.

During the three-week season a total of eighteen concerts are offered every evening but Monday. In the tradition of many of the European music festivals, concerts are scheduled in various interesting, unique, and picturesque locations: Shelburne Farms, Shelburne, with its beautiful English country Tudor mansion built in 1887, its south porch and coach barn; the *M. V. Champlain,* a thirty-ton ferry boat which features cruise concerts on Lake Champlain; Mead Chapel, Middlebury College, Middlebury, built of marble in the turn-of-the-century revivalism style; Stratton Mountain Lodge; Saint Monica Church, Barre, built in 1887 with seating for 675 concertgoers; Show Barn, Burlington, has a 1500-seat concert hall and is part of the College of Agriculture at the University of Vermont; and Recital Hall, University of Vermont, used for small ensembles and recitals and accommodates 300 persons; Royall Tyler Theater, Cathedral Church of Saint Paul, and Saint Joseph's Church, all in Burlington.

The Vermont Mozart Festival's official residence is in Burlington, located in the northwestern part of the state and lying between the famous Green Mountains and the majestic Adirondacks. Not long ago, the festival was perhaps the Vermonters' best-kept secret, but no longer, for the word and the music are getting around!

For information write to: Vermont Mozart Festival, Post Office Box 512, Burlington, Vermont 05402. Telephone: (802) 862-7352.

For accommodations write: Lake Champlain Regional Chamber of Commerce, 131 Main Street, Burlington, Vermont 05401. Telephone: (802) 863-3489.

SHENANDOAH VALLEY MUSIC FESTIVAL
Orkney Springs, Virginia
Mid-July for three weekends

One of the legendary musical figures of our time, Dr. Richard Johannes Lert, has been presiding over the Shenandoah Valley Music Festival as artistic director since its beginning in 1963. Previously conductor of the Pasadena Symphony for over thirty-eight years, he retired in 1972 and devoted more time to conducting at the festival. Dr. Lert, affectionately called "Dr. Hans" by his colleagues, is respected and revered by his staff, students, and audiences. Born in Austria in 1885, he had Arthur Nikisch as his mentor, and thus Dr. Lert, who celebrated his ninety-third birthday in 1978, is considered the last living link to the conducting tradition of Nikisch.

The American Symphony Orchestra League began holding conductor workshops, called the Eastern Institute of Orchestra Studies, in Orkney Springs, Virginia in 1960. Helen M. Thompson of the League and Col. Robert Benchoff, headmaster of the Massanutten Military Academy, decided that if music of such high quality were being produced, the local residents should benefit. Thus, in 1963, the Shenandoah Valley Music Festival was officially established; the League supplied a symphony orchestra made up of professional musicians from all over the country, and the public was invited to attend the concerts. The festival is actually an intensive three-week workshop session whereby a selected number of young conductors gain experience under the tutelage of Dr. Lert and his colleagues and a full symphony orchestra. The capable staff who have been assisting Dr. Lert since the first year of the festival are Phillip Spurgeon, Robert Kreis, and Samuel Jones. The festival orchestra, as the basic ensemble, performs symphonic and chamber music, and for variety a pops concert has been added to the programming.

Orkney Springs, Virginia, is tucked away in the Shenandoah Valley range. Once a bustling resort area, it is now a quiet, peaceful community which comes alive during the weeks of the festival. Concerts scheduled Fridays, Saturdays, and Sundays are performed in the majestic, historic nineteenth-century Orkney Springs Hotel pavilion. The unique old hotel is set among huge trees, and as the pavilion is open on all sides, the 700 patrons within have a lovely vista of the Massanutten Mountains. For those who prefer lawn seating, there is space outside for an additional 1,000 patrons. The state of Virginia offers numerous historic sights, some of the finest scenery in the East, and a wide range of special events from Civil War battle reenactments, Apple Blossom festivals to old-time fiddler's conventions. The Shenandoah Music Festival is indeed a special event which contains cultural, historical, and scenic significance!

For information write: Shenandoah Valley Music Festival, P.O. Box 12, Woodstock, Virginia 22664. Telephone: (703) 459-3396.

For accommodations write to: Woodstock Chamber of Commerce, Inc., 134 North Main Street, Woodstock, Virginia 22664. Telephone: (703) 459-2542.

WOLF TRAP FARM
Vienna, Virginia
*June to the first week in September
for thirteen weeks*

Wolf Trap Farm, sixteen miles southwest of Washington, D.C., in the foothills of the Blue Ridge Mountains, was so named because of traps that were set for the wolves that made the region dangerous in the 1700s, and for which rewards of one hundred-pound weights of tobacco were paid for each wolf head! Filene Center, an open amphitheater—is a graceful, sloping wooden structure standing ten stories high—amidst rolling hills and grassy pastureland. The original building burned to the ground three and a half months before the scheduled opening concert in 1971. A benefit performance by the New York Philharmonic helped make up the loss, and the center was rebuilt and opened on time. Inside the dramatic wooden-timbered structure, some 3,500 may choose seats under protection of the amphitheater roof, and another 3,000 may favor the sloping lawn outside. Wolf Trap offers every kind of music, including symphonic works, chamber music, opera, operettas, instrumental and vocal recitals, dance programs, jazz, folk, ragtime, bluegrass, and country music.

Julius Rudel, present artistic advisor, is often engaged as a guest conductor, as well as other notables: Sarah Caldwell, Aaron Copland, Mstislav Rostropovich, Henry Mancini, Eugene Ormandy, Raymond Leppard, Arthur Fiedler, and Gunther Schuller.

The list of internationally famous vocal and instrumental soloists and performing groups is numerous and impressive. It is at Wolf Trap that singers Tony Bennett, Martina Arroyo, James Bowman, Johnny Cash, Ella Fitzgerald, James McCracken, Anna Moffo, John Reardon, Beverly Sills, and Shirley Verrett have starred, along with instrumentalists Victor Borge, Van Cliburn, Yehudi Menuhin, Carlos Montoya, Rafael Orozco, Jean-Pierre Rampal, and André Watts. Dance ensembles of world renown have appeared—Eliot Feld Ballet, Martha Graham Dance Company, Joffrey Ballet, London Contemporary Dance Theater, and Stuttgart Ballet, and countless more. The Metropolitan Opera

Company with a star-studded cast is an important ingredient of the festival, as well as the Wolf Trap Opera Company.

The other facilities in the park are the Theatre-in-the-Woods, used for daily programs such as mime and puppet shows for children and adults; a Concert Shell for Sunday band concerts and special events such as the National Folk Festival; Meadow Tent for theater events and a lecture hall; and Composers' Cottage, a quiet retreat and location for musicians to create and compose.

Wolf Trap Farm, donated by Mrs. Jouett Shouse, and designated by Congress as the first national park dedicated to the performing arts, under the jurisdiction of the National Park Service, opened in July, 1971. The Wolf Trap Foundation, an organization created by the Secretary of the Interior, oversees and determines the artistic and educational programming of Wolf Trap. It also manages Wolf Trap Opera Company, Wolf Trap Orchestra, and some master classes. The Foundation's philosophy, under the inspiration of Mrs. Shouse, is to present varied programs designed to attract audiences of widely differing tastes.

As they say at Wolf Trap, "Life's too short and winter's too long not to enjoy the summer at Wolf Trap!"

Write for tickets to: Wolf Trap Farm Park for the Performing Arts, 1624 Trap Road, Vienna, Virginia 22180. Telephone: (703) 938-3800 or 938-3810.

For accommodations information write to: Chamber of Commerce, 302 Maple Avenue, Vienna, Virginia 22180. Telephone: (703) 281-1333.

MUSIC UNDER THE STARS
Milwaukee, Wisconsin
*Third week in June to the second week in August
for eight weeks*

A major and very popular summer music and dance event in the Milwaukee area is Music Under the Stars. The series began in 1938 under the co-sponsorship of the Milwaukee County Park Commission and the Journal Company. All concerts are offered to the public without charge. (Coupons appear in the

Milwaukee Journal and *Milwaukee Sentinel* newspapers and are redeemable for reserved seat performances.) The programs range from orchestral music, selected movements from symphonies or short classical works, to fully staged operas, operettas, dance ensembles, pops, and evenings with mixed musical presentations. Maestro John-David Anello conducts both of the major performing groups of the series — the Milwaukee Symphony Orchestra and the Milwaukee Florentine Opera. As the programming emphasizes operatic music and musicals, often stars from the Chicago Lyric Opera, the Metropolitan Opera, New York City Opera, and other major opera companies are invited guests. Prominent artists in recent years have included singers Karan Armstrong, Aaron Bergell, Anthony Becerril, Alan Crofoot, Rosalind Elias, Richard Fredericks, John Gary, William Lewis, Leigh Munro, Nicolas Flagello, William Walker, and William Warfield.

John-David Anello, music director and conductor of the Music Under the Stars series, a native Milwaukean, a cultural leader, and a gentleman who is deeply involved in many civic and musical activities in the city, has been affectionaltely called, "Milwaukee's Mr. Music," "Mr. Pops," and "Mr. Florentine." A left-handed conductor (one of very few in the conductorial profession), Maestro Anello maintains it is a help as the beat may be more easily followed by the first violinist!

For full symphonic concerts, operas, and large productions, the Emil Blatz Temple of Music in Washington Park is used. Performers are under cover of a huge acoustical shell, similar in appearance to the Hollywood Bowl shell, and 16,000 attendees may be seated outside "under the stars." The shell was donated to the city for the opening series in 1938 by Emil Blatz, a brewing magnate and philanthropist. Other performances are given over the entire county in many different parks such as Humboldt Park Chalet, Mitchell Park, Carl Zeidler Park, Kosciuszko Park, the County Zoo, Whitnall Park, and Pere Marquette Park. So from minuet to madrigal, martial to mezzo moderato, Milwaukee's music and its master pleases them one and all!

For information write to: Music Under the Stars, Milwaukee County Park Commission, 4420 West Vliet Street, Milwaukee, Wisconsin 53208. Telephone: (414) 278-4389.

For accommodations write to: Milwaukee Convention and Visitors Bureau, 828 North Broadway, Milwaukee, Wisconsin 53202. Telephone: (414) 273-3950.

PENINSULA MUSIC FESTIVAL
Fish Creek, Wisconsin
First week in August for two weeks

Fish Creek doesn't sound exactly where one might expect to find a high-quality music festival, but there is one there, and it is thriving. Perhaps it has not received the publicity of larger, well-known musical events; yet it attains a high level of performance to match some of the more publicized and popular summer festivals. Dr. Thor Johnson, music director and conductor of the Cincinnati Symphony Orchestra and the Peninsula Arts Association started the Peninsula Music Festival in 1953. Dr. Johnson, a native of Wisconsin, spent happy childhood days in Door County, and dreamed one day of bringing good classical music to the region. Under his leadership, emphasis was placed on the less familiar music rather than the well-tried standards; many new works were commissioned, and world and United States premieres were programmed. A few of the composers who in recent years have had their works commissioned or premiered are Leslie Bassett, Cecil Effinger, Gene Hemmer, John Hilliard, Gail Kubik, Verne Reynolds, Wallingford Riegger, Alan Stout, and Paul Whear.

The basic ensemble for the festival is a forty-piece orchestra composed of professional musicians in the area. Guest soloists are invited, and Dr. Johnson, whenever feasible, invited artists with "Wisconsin roots." Among some of the artist who have appeared in recent years are vocalists, Helen Boatwright, Patricia Brooks, Dominic Cossa, Jan DeGaetani, Dale Duesing, Donald Gramm, Joanna Simon, and Eleanor Steber; pianists, John Browning, Malcolm Frager, Claude Frank, Frank Glazer, Gary Graffmann, Hans Richter-Haaser, Leonard Pennario, Garrick Ohlsson, and Rosalyn Tureck; violinists, Sidney Harth, Paul Kling, Daniel Majeske, Oscar Perria, and Charles Treger. Upon Dr. Johnson's untimely death in 1975, a number of guest conductors were invited to the festival. In 1978, Michael Charry, conductor of the Nashville Symphony Orchestra, took over the position as conductor and music director of the Peninsula Music Festival.

The concerts are given in the 750-seat Gibraltar Auditorium in Fish Creek in Door County. The community is situated on a peninsula stretching out forty miles and separating the waters of Lake Michigan and Green Bay. The area is a bustling and popular resort in the summertime, as people are attracted to the quaint historic towns, the picturesque fishing villages, and little harbors. Often called, "The Cape Cod of the Midwest," Fish Creek and its surrounding area have been for many years a retreat for artists, musicians, and writers. The natural beauty of the region, the invigorating climate, and the atmosphere are all conducive to making beautiful music, and the Peninsula Music Festival does!

For tickets and information write to: Peninsula Music Festival, Pioneer School House, Ephraim Door County, Wisconsin 54211. Telephone: (414) 854-4060.

For accommodations write to: Door County Chamber of Commerce, Green Bay Road, Sturgeon Bay, Wisconsin 55235. Telephone: (414) 743-4456.

GRAND TETON MUSIC FESTIVAL
Jackson, Wyoming
Mid-July to mid-August for six weeks

Set among trees and a mountain brook on the lower slope of the Grand Tetons, one of America's most beautiful mountain ranges, the amphitheater in which this festival of symphonies and chamber works is held is noted for its excellent acoustics and intimate atmosphere. The Grand Teton Music Festival has in addition to seven Saturday night symphonic concerts, instrumental and vocal recitals, such special events as "Watermelon Concerts," with a watermelon social after some of the chamber music programs; "Music in the Present Tense" presents contemporary music and a lecture and discussion led by a resident composer, and Marathon Concerts, which begin at 7:00 P.M., and have been known to continue for as long as twelve hours straight!

Founded in 1962 to provide a workshop-seminar environment for the continuing development of outstanding musicians, the festival has gained national recognition for its high standards in performance and for its imaginative and varied programming. The ninety-six-member festival orchestra is composed of many musicians from the Philharmonic Orchestra of Philadelphia, as well as from many first-class musical institutions throughout the country. Ling Tung, music director of the Grand Teton Music Festival Philharmonia Orchestra is also conductor of the Philharmonic Orchestra of Philadelphia and is credited with bringing the festival to Teton Village and inspiring the construction of the Festival Hall.

Musical performances have featured singers Katherine and Kristine Ciesinski, Phyllis Curtin, John Stewart, and Julia Emoed-Wallace; pianists Steven De Groote, Richard Goode, Diedre Irons, and Monique Duphil; cellist Barbara Haffner, violinist William Henry; violist Nardo Poy; and composers-in-residence David Amram, Karel Husa, Joseph Castaldo, and Roger Ruggeri.

Concerts are given Tuesday through Saturday evenings in the 830-seat Festival Hall built in 1973. The hall has seating similar to a Greek amphitheater with semicircular rows which rise sharply from the stage.

Teton Village is in the Grand Teton National Park, seventeen miles northwest of Jackson in the northwestern part of Wyoming. This is one of the most unique and spectacular areas in the country with its 12,000-foot mountains in the Grand Teton National Park and the Snake River, and offers unlimited recreational opportunities to sports-minded visitors and nature-lovers.

"Only music could make it more beautiful" is indeed an apt slogan for this fine musicmaking in the mountains.

Write for tickets to: Grand Teton Music Festival, Post Office Box 20, Teton Village, Wyoming 83025. Telephone: (307) 733-3050.

For accommodations write to: Teton Village Resort Association, Teton Village, Wyoming 83025. Telephone: (307) 733-4005. Or Jackson Hole Chamber of Commerce, Post Office Box E, Jackson, Wyoming 83001. Telephone: (307) 733-3316.

For additional classical performances, see Index for following:

Grant Park Concerts, Illinois

OPERA

C. Elke '78

INSPIRATION POINT FINE ARTS COLONY FESTIVAL
Eureka Springs, Arkansas
Mid-June to the last week in July for six weeks

Eureka Springs may rightfully boast of being one of the oldest resorts in the Ozark Mountains, of having some of the most beautiful scenery in the South, and of hosting one of the most authentic folk festivals in the country, the Ozark Folk Festival; but it should also be proud of a fine, progressive opera workshop within its environs at Inspiration Point Colony. In 1950, Dr. Henry Hobart founded the opera workshop under the co-sponsorship of the Federation of Music Clubs in Arkansas, Illinois, Kansas, Missouri, and Oklahoma. Dr. Isaac Van Grove was appointed artistic director the first season, and he has been the motivating force behind the "Colony" ever since. Dr. Van Grove's musical accomplishments prior to his association with the Colony were varied and impressive. He was accompanist for Mary Garden; toured with Grace Moore, the glamourous soprano of stage, screen, and opera; worked closely with the famous German impresario Max Reinhardt in New York and Hollywood; and was music director and conductor of the Chicago and Cincinnati Operas!

The Inspiration Point Fine Arts Colony has workshops in opera, dance, scene design, instrumental, music theory, piano, private voice, costume design, and other fine arts. Students and faculty, which total less than fifty, come from all over the country and, because of the experience and training they receive, often return year after year. A few of the faculty are Roger Cantrell, Carroll Freeman, Errol and Anna Haun, Kris Hanley, Lynn Hamilton, Ronald Wheeler, Cole Roberts, and Jeanice Hobart. Towards the end of the six-week session, students and faculty stage four operas—each are performed two or three times, and the public is invited to attend. The repertoire ranges from the familiar classics to lesser-known operas, and Dr. Van Grove, also an accomplished composer, has had several of his operas performed in recent seasons: *The Shining Chalice, The Prodigal Wandering Years,* and *The Miracle of Our Lady.* Performances are held in the indoor pavilion on the campus which seats 300 patrons, and if weather and repertoire permit, occasionally operas are performed outside.

For tickets and information write to: Inspiration Point Fine Arts Colony Route 2, Box 348AA, Eureka Springs, Arkansas 72632. Telephone: (501) 253-8595.

For accommodations write to: Chamber of Commerce, Post Office Box 551, Eureka Springs, Arkansas 72632. Telephone: (501) 253-8737.

SPRING OPERA THEATER
San Francisco, California
Spring for four weeks

Imaginative, innovative, and adventuresome are a few of the words used to describe the San Francisco Spring Opera Theater. A youngster in comparison to other opera festivals, SPOT, as it is called by the natives, has come a long way in a short time. Inspiration for Spring Opera came in 1960 when Lillian Cuenin, Marie-Luise Adams, and William Kent III, decided that rather than trying to save the financially-ailing Cosmopolitan Opera, it would be better to start a new kind of opera company to augment the already-successful San Francisco Opera Company. Since its inception, the goals of SPOT have been to provide performance opportunities for young American operatic talent, to produce opera in English at popular prices, and to introduce audiences to a varied repertoire of new works, revivals, and little-known classics. SPOT has "soft pedaled" the star system and concentrates on developing talent. As a result, a number of relatively unknown singers have gained experience with SPOT and furthered their musical careers. Some of these vocalist have been Maria Ewing, Richard Fredricks, Marilyn Horne, James King, Chester Ludgin, Janis Martin, Leona Mitchell, Ken Remo, George Shirley, Alan Titus, Norman Treigle, and Frederica Von Stade.

Spring Opera's orchestra is composed of members of the San Francisco Symphony, Oakland Symphony, and other professional musicians. Many guest conductors, directors, and designers are invited throughout the season, and may turn out to be the next superstars! Kurt Herbert Adler, general director of the San Francisco Opera, has also been general director of Spring Opera since its beginning. In 1971, Spring Opera decided to alter its format, renamed itself Spring Opera Theater, and emphasized drama as well as opera. The productions moved from the San Francisco Opera House to the 1752-seat Curran Theatre, a more intimate setting. A thrust stage was added, extending over the orchestra pit, thus permitting dynamic contact between the singers and the audience. The end result is that performances are both an operatic and theater experience.

The stage direction and productions are sometimes contemporary, when appropriate, and often filled with surprises. Patrons recall particularly Donizetti's comedy, *Don Pasquale* which was set in San Francisco on California Street at the beginning of this century. The "dialogue" matched the times. During the opera, tenor John Alexander was late making his entrance and came rushing on the stage, breathless, but able to sing out, "I'm here, Uncle!" Whereupon Stephen West bellowed back, "You're late!" A surprise for the cast as well as for the audience!

Some of the West Coast and United States opera premieres presented by Spring Opera Theater have been Benjamin Britten's *Death in Venice*, Kurt Weill's *Mahagonny* and Viktor Ullman's *Emperor of Atlantis*. A few of the many interesting revivals and contemporary operas staged in recent years have been *Carry Nation, Elegy for Young Lovers, Julius Caesar, Titus, L'Ormindo, Of Mice and Men, Orfeo, Saint Matthew's Passion, Turn of the Screw*, and *Viva La Mama*.

It is not pure chance that San Francisco is one of the outstanding opera centers in the United States and the world, for with musical happenings such as Spring Opera Theater, it has been able to attract a much broader spectrum of opera lovers and performers to their mutual benefit.

For information and tickets write to: Spring Opera Theater, War Memorial Opera House, San Francisco, California 94102. Telephone: (415) 431-1463.

For accommodations write to: San Francisco Convention and Visitors Bureau, 1390 Market Street, San Francisco, California 94102. Telephone: (415) 626-5500.

VERDI FESTIVAL
San Diego, California
Third week in June for two to three weeks

San Diego is a lively cultural city with its Old Globe Theatre Shakespeare productions, the Fine Arts Gallery, San Diego Opera, San Diego Ballet, and San Diego Symphony, and now it is the first city in the country and, in fact, the world, to initiate a full-fledged Giuseppe Verdi Festival. The focus of the festival in the next decade will be to provide a performance and experimental center where innovative ways of producing Verdi's works may be explored. Its plans for this ten-year period include all of Verdi's twenty-six operas, his string quartet, art songs, and his three principal choral works. Seminars, master classes, workshops, and films will be offered during the festival in hopes that musicians, vocalists, and concertgoers gain a deeper appreciation and understanding of Verdi the man, and Verdi's works.

The festival, sponsored by the San Diego Opera, has as its music director, Tito Capobianco, who is also general director of the San Diego Opera. The San Diego Opera Orchestra and the San Diego Symphonic Chorale are the main ensembles for the performances and top-rank guest conductors and vocalists are invited for the festival.

The 1978 season entitled "Prologue to a Verdi Festival" included three performances of *Aida* and one of the Requiem. The artists who appeared were Antonio Tauriello, conductor; Martina Arroyo, Carlo Bini, Philip Booth, Robert Hale, Norman Millelmann, and Carol Wyatt, vocalists.

The 1979 offerings are *La Traviata* and the American premiere of *I'Lombardi,* one of Verdi's earliest operas. This was written in 1843 and is considered his first patriotic opera, expressing as it does the feelings he and his compatriots had under Austrian occupation. Artists performing for these operas are Carlo Bergonzi, Christina Deutekon, Paul Plishka, Rico Serbo, Diane Soviero, and Vittorio Terranova, vocalists; Marizio Arena and Hans Vonk, conductors. Tito Capobianco directs *I'Lombardi* and Charles Nelson Reilly, *La Traviata.*

The operas are staged in the 3,000-seat civic auditorium in downtown San Diego, and the recitals, seminars, workshops, and master classes are held in various areas around the city — plazas, Balboa Park, and on campuses of nearby universities.

Warm waters, soft winds, and the bountiful sun have made San Diego a mecca for surfers, swimmers, sailors, the sports enthusiasts, and for just plain tourists. Now romantic arias, dramatic duets, and melodic recitals will beckon opera buffs, Verdi devotees, and in fact music lovers of any conviction, to San Diego's Verdi Festival.

For information write to: Verdi Festival, c/o San Diego Opera, Post Office Box 988, San Diego, California 92112. Telephone: (714) 232-7636.

For accommodations write to: San Diego Convention and Visitors Bureau, 1200 Third Avenue, San Diego, California 92101. Telephone: (714) 232-3101.

CENTRAL CITY SUMMER FESTIVAL
Central City, Colorado
First week in July to the end of August for eight weeks

"The richest square mile on earth." This was Central City in its heyday, for from the discovery of gold in 1859 to the panic in 1893, that "square mile" produced more than eighty million dollars. Since those days when the "streets were lined with silver and gold," the people in Central City have been devoted to the cultural arts. Miners worked hard during the day, but the evenings found them not only in saloons, but also at the theater! With this colorful heritage of cultural enthusiasm, it is not surprising that the Opera Festival inaugurated in 1932 was the first summer opera festival in the country, and the first to advocate opera sung in English. Continuing this tradition, the Festival regularly commissions translations of major works into English and produces new operas.

Artists engaged from the Metropolitan Opera Company, New York City Opera, and from other major companies in the country have been Charles Bressler, John Ferrante, Jerome Hines, Spiro Malas, Regina Resnik, Judith Raskin, Norman Treigle, Veronica Tyler, and Benita Valente to name a few. Young Artists Apprentice Programs stages one opera during the season, and other musical events such as performances of light opera or jazz groups at the close of the opera season.

High in the Rocky Mountains, a short forty miles west of Denver, Central City still offers many reminders of the days when gold was discovered and thousands of prospectors swarmed into the community. The historic Teller House, once the city's grand hotel, built in 1872, had thirty solid silver bricks placed into the pavement before the house in honor of President Ulysses S. Grant's visit. What better way to be reminded of the city's golden past than to attend a performance at the Opera House? Built in 1878 and described as a very "democratic house—no boxes, just main floor and balcony," it has been restored to its original Victorian elegance with beautiful murals and crystal chandeliers. The hall has excellent acoustics and seats 800 patrons in "kitchen chairs."

Central City has staged three premieres, the most popular being *The Ballad of Baby Doe* by Douglas Moore. The opera follows with great historical fidelity the career of the wealthy silver king, Horace Tabor, his involvement in the Matchless Silver Mine and his infatuation with Baby Doe from Central City. Other premiered operas have been *Of Mice and Men* by Carlisle Floyd, *Scipio Africanus* by Cavalli and *Midsummer Night's Dream* by Benjamin Britten. Following a closing performance, the festival audience has a tradition of tossing carnations at the cast. When Britten's opera, *Midsummer Night's Dream* closed the 1974 season, there were literally garlands and blankets of flowers covering the stage in special tribute to this excellent production!

For tickets write to: Central City Opera House Association, University Building, 910 16th Street, Suite 636, Denver, Colorado 80202. Telephone: (303) 623-7167.

For accommodations write to: Denver Chamber of Commerce, 1301 Welton Street, Denver, Colorado 80202. Telephone: (303) 534-3211.

COLORADO OPERA FESTIVAL
Colorado Springs, Colorado
Mid-June to the first week in August for seven weeks

"Colorado Opera Festival sides with the angels in trying at least one challenging work each year." This indeed states the purpose of the festival—to provide professional and innovative productions of important and sometimes rarely performed works which are chosen on the basis of their musical and dramatic worth. In keeping with this goal, the 1971 season included a world premiere—revival of Traetta's *Il Cavaliere Errante,* last performed in 1804; and rarely performed operas were featured in the 1973 season with Kurt Weill's *The Rise and Fall of The City of Mahogonny,* and in the 1978 season, with Handel's *Xerxes.* The season offers three or four operas with the majority sung in English.

One of the festival's founders, Donald P. Jenkins, conductor and artistic director since its inception, is very enthusiastic about opera in English. He searches for workable and interesting translations so that the color and cadence of the original language is not lost. When asked if he ever heard of a composer refusing to have his opera translated into another language, Jenkins commented, "Puccini was glad to assist in translating *Tosca* and *Boheme* into French. Wagner approved of performances of the *Ring (Der Ring Des Nibelungen)* into Hungarian, Russian, French, Danish, and Italian. Even Verdi was shocked to hear that the Paris Opera intended to put on *Otello* in Italian and urged the director to present it in French!"

The festival started in 1970 as a cooperative endeavor of

Colorado College and the Colorado Choral Society, and functions as a professional opera company and an opera workshop in residence at the college during the summer. The singers and production artists come from major opera companies in the country, as well as from the Rocky Mountain area. An important segment of the season is the apprentice programs whereby young singers receive not only voice lessons, instructions in acting and stage movements, but also sing minor and major roles in the Opera Festival productions. Some of the featured guest singers have been Herbert Beattie, Gary Glaze, Hilda Harris, Elizabeth Hynes, Erik Townsend, Beverly Evans, Herbert Eckhoff, Sandra Walker, and Paul Aquino. The operas are staged in the 800-seat Armstrong Theatre on the campus of Colorado College in Colorado Springs.

For tickets and information write to: The Colorado Opera Festival, Colorado College, Armstrong Hall, Colorado Springs, Colorado 80903. Telephone: (303) 473-2233.

For accommodations write to: Chamber of Commerce, Chase Stone Center, Colorado Springs, Colorado 80903. Telephone: (303) 635-1551.

SANTA FE OPERA FESTIVAL
Santa Fe, New Mexico
First week in July to the last week in August for eight weeks

Nagasaki in New Mexico? Relying on the natural scenery for dramatic effects, opera devotees attending a 1974 performance of *Madame Butterfly* felt as though they were seeing the lights of the Japanese city, when in fact, the rear doors of the stage had been thrown open and the sparkling lights of a New Mexican town shone below!

Going to Santa Fe is a total cultural experience for it offers beautiful scenery, historic sights, fine art displays and workshops, an interesting blend of cultural heritages, and an opera company that has since its beginning achieved world recognition for its outstanding professional standards.

The inspiration for Santa Fe Opera has been director and conductor, John Crosby. A man of great perception and energy, he saw that the physical and cultural climate of Santa Fe was perfect for opera and was able to turn his vision into a reality in the summer of 1957. Santa Fe stages its own productions of operas—the majority sung in English, sometimes with international stars, but more often with emphasis on new and young singers. The fare is a combination of old classics and new untried works, and there have been twenty American or world premieres in twenty-one years! Some of the operas premiered have been Igor Stravinsky's *Persephone,* Carlisle Floyd's *Wuthering Heights,* Luciano Berio's *Opera,* Dmitri Shostakovich's *The Nose,* Paul Hindemith's *Cardillac,* Gian-Carlo Menotti's *Help! Help! The Globolinks,* and Heitor Villa-Lobos' *Yerma.*

The opera house, perched on a mesa between the Jemez and Sangre de Cristo mountains, is six miles from Santa Fe and is a striking, dramatic modern structure of redwood and stucco. The seating is *alfresco,* and as the evenings are cool, patrons are advised that warm clothing rules over elegance. The house has excellent acoustics and provides seating for 1,765 patrons, the majority of whom are under cover of a huge roof. The original opera house burned to the ground one evening in 1967, taking most of the season's sets, costumes, and music. A massive effort by citizens and artists permitted the opera season to continue despite this tragedy. The following night, the opera was staged in the high school gymnasium, and a few days later, construction began on the new existing opera house.

An important aspect of Santa Fe Opera is the Apprentice Program for Artists established to help young singers in the difficult transition from student life to a professional career. Young artists are trained in voice, drama, dance, and costume design, and perform during the season. Many who have appeared with the opera have later become distinguished soloists in major opera houses in Europe and America. Some who have made their American or Santa Fe debuts are Sheri Greenawald, James Bowman, Ellen Shade, Jean Kraft, Phillip Booth, John Reardon, Judith Raskin, Patricia Brooks, and George Shirley, to name a few.

The repertoire includes five or six operas performed nightly, except Sundays, during the eight-week season.

Visitors can explore Santa Fe's various old buildings, art galleries, and workshops where local artisans are at work. There are also many day excursions to pueblos such as Taos Pueblo, San Ildefonso, Santa Clara, Tesuque, San Juan, and many other small, but fascinating, villages in the area. The colorful Spanish and Indian heritage of this area—the lingering visible evidence of its history—somehow permeates the spirit and makes the musical experience more vital and poignant.

For tickets write to: Santa Fe Opera, Post Office Box 2408, Santa Fe, New Mexico 87501. Telephone: (505) 982-3851.

For accommodations write to: Santa Fe Chamber of Commerce, Post Office Box 1928, Santa Fe, New Mexico 87501. Telephone: (505) 983-7317.

LAKE GEORGE OPERA FESTIVAL
Glens Falls, New York
Mid-July to the last week in August for six weeks

Alva Henderson's opera, *The Last of the Mohicans* opened in home territory when it premiered in 1977. Patrons in Glens Falls, New York were treated to an evening of excitement (blood and thunder!) as historical events unfolded before their eyes in a familiar setting . . . the caves of Glens Falls in the Adirondack Mountains!

The Lake George Opera Festival emphasizes opera in English, the use of young and talented singers, and a repertoire which includes modern innovative works as well as the familiar standards. Supportive of American composers, it has in its short history staged six world and American premieres. The thirty-five-piece orchestra is composed of musicians from the Boston, New York Philharmonic, and Albany symphonies, and the chorus is drawn from two groups in the "opera family"—the Opera Workshop and the Young Resident Artists Program.

The guest artists who have appeared over the years have included Ronald Hedlund, Theresa Treadway, Henry Price, Herbert Beattie, William Parker, Nicholas Di Virgilio, John Sandor, and Barbara Hocher.

The opera festival was started in 1962 by Fred Patrick, a man with great talent and enthusiasm for the project. Upon his untimely death in 1965, David Lloyd, a tenor singing at the festival, took over as general director, a position he has held ever since, and in 1976 his son, David Thomas Lloyd, became artistic director. In addition to the familiar opera repertoire, the festival has included some new and interesting productions — *The Mother of Us All, Faust Counter Faust, Summer and Smoke,* and *The Crucible.* The first years the operas were staged in a small, open-sided barnlike structure, and patrons sat on park benches. The rain often drowned out the piano accompaniment and the singers. In 1965, the opera productions were relocated to the 876-seat Queensberry High School auditorium in Glens Falls for the majority of the programs. Some of the opera performances are given each year in Albany at the State University of New York and at Lake Placid Center for Music, Drama, and Art. "Opera on the Lake" cruises are a novel feature of the festival! Aboard the historic ship, *Mohican,* singers and patrons alike enjoy an evening of sunset, spirits, and song.

For tickets and information write to: Lake George Opera Festival, P.O. Box 425, Glens Falls, New York 12801. Telephone: (518) 793-3858.

For accommodations write to: Adirondack Chamber of Commerce, 206 Glen Street, Glens Falls, New York 12801. Telephone: (518) 798-1761.

CINCINNATI SUMMER OPERA FESTIVAL
Cincinnati, Ohio
Mid-June to the end of July for six weeks

"Zoo Opera" in Cincinnati did not feature performing bears and seals, but this affectionate name came obout as the Cincinnati Summer Opera was performed in the Cincinnati zoo for over fifty-one years from its first season until 1972! Ralph Lyford is credited with starting the opera in 1920, thus establishing the first summer opera in the country and the second oldest continuing opera in the nation (the Metropolitan is the oldest). In the early days, performances in the zoo competed with an already-popular ice show scheduled the same evenings as the opera. In order to preserve attendance at the opera, a forty-five minute intermission was arranged each night, and opera patrons "had their cake"—opera plus the ice skating show! This "double billing" continued until 1932 when the ice show disbanded.

The season's format under general director James de Blasis, has been to engage well-known singers, designers, and conductors; to stage five or six better-known operas with two or three performances; and to present special performances for young audiences. The Cincinnati Symphony Orchestra members make up the opera orchestra. In the past, Chicago and Metropolitan Opera houses provided the chorus, but presently local talent is used. Many careers have been launched at the summer opera as artists made their operatic debuts: Rise Stevens, Mary Costa, Robert Weede, John Alexander, and Jan Peerce. Many well-known singers have appeared over the years: Ezio Pinza, Anna Moffo, Johanna Meier, Sherrill Milnes, Phyllis Curtin,

Norman Treigle, Robert Merrill, Elizabeth Schwarzkopf, Frank Guarrera, Richard Tucker, Blanche Thebom, Dorothy Kirsten, Beverly Sills, Richard Woitach, Leonard Warren, Frances Bible, Beverly Wolff, and many others.

In 1972, the Cincinnati Summer Opera moved to the Music Hall, considered one of the most beautiful and functional opera houses in the world. Covering a city block, the Music Hall is in the center of downtown Cincinnati and has undergone massive renovation since its opening in 1878. The refurbished auditorium, seating 3,602 patrons, reopened in 1972 and features beautiful Czechoslovakian chandeliers and French ornamentation.

Write for tickets to: Cincinnati Opera, Music Hall, 1241 Elm Street, Cincinnati, Ohio 45210. Telephone: (513) 621-1919.

For accommodations write to: Cincinnati Convention and Visitors' Bureau, 200 West Fifth Street, Cincinnati, Ohio 44210. Telephone: (513) 621-2142.

PACIFIC NORTHWEST FESTIVAL
Seattle, Washington
July for two weeks

The *Ring* today; tomorrow, the "Festival of the Forest!" Seattle is thinking big and is proud to be the first city in the Western Hemisphere to produce a Wagnerian festival with *Der Ring des Nibelungen.* Seattle was once considered a provincial city, but the 1962 World's Fair gave residents the opportunity to enjoy the finest cultural events in the world. They developed an appetite for more, and they are doing something about it. The inspiration, imagination, and force behind the Pacific Northwest Festival is a gentle but determined man, Glynn Ross, general director of the Seattle Opera. Ross, who has been called, "the greatest promoter since Barnum and Bailey," paved the way for the festival by obtaining large grants which permitted productions of one of the four operas in the *Ring* each season since 1973. The following year, the Washington State Legislature appropriated a handsome sum to develop a Wagnerian festival. Thus, Pacific Northwest Festival was officially launched in 1975, the realization of a long dream for Glynn Ross, the Seattle Opera, its patrons, and opera enthusiasts all over the country and the world.

The Seattle Opera Company presents the four Wagnerian

operas in *Der Ring des Nibelungen* within one week's time. This is the traditional manner in which the *Ring* is regularly performed at the Wagner Festspielhaus in Bayreuth, Germany. The following week, the Seattle Opera Company repeats the cycle in English—a feat that no other company in the world has accomplished! People have come from all over the world to attend the *Ring,* and to accommodate the foreign visitors, the 1979 program announcement is printed in German, French, Spanish, Japanese, and English!

Music director since the first year has been Henry Holt, who engages not only young singers at the start of their careers, but the very finest Wagnerian performers in the world. Past seasons have welcomed Herbert Becker, Ingrid Bjoner, Philip Booth, Marvellee Cariaga, Margaret Curphey, Paul Crook, Raimund Herincx, Rudolph Holtenau, Richard Kness, Johanna Meier, Alberto Remedios, Malcolm Rivers, and Ute Vinzing. All operas are performed in the 3,017-seat Seattle Opera House, the former Civic Auditorium which was remodeled for the 1962 World's Fair.

Everyone who has met Glynn Ross has a favorite Glynn Ross story. The author is no exception, for in the early 1970s, she was privileged to hear Mr. Ross's tape recording of his five-year-old daughter telling the long and very complicated story of the *Ring* in vivid detail. It was told with the childish animation and enthusiasm that one might expect of a tale of *The Wizard of Oz* or *Little Red Riding Hood.* Ross maintains that while most children were reading stories from *Grimms Fairy Tales,* his children delighted in the opera epic, *The Ring!*

Ross dreams, schemes, and has been hard at work developing plans for a Pacific Northwest "Festival in the Forest." He foresees turning a large wooded area (which he calls a forest) outside of Seattle into the site of year-around activity with a larger Wagnerian series and presentations of other performing arts. The "forest" has already been pledged by the Weyerhauser Company, and if anyone can make *The Ring* sing in the "Forest," it is Glynn Ross!

For information write to: Seattle Opera/Pacific Northwest Wagner Festival, Post Office Box 9248, Seattle, Washington 98109. Telephone: (206) 447-4700.

For accommodations write to: Seattle Convention and Visitor's Bureau, 1815 Seventh Avenue, Seattle, Washington 98101. Telephone: (206) 447-7273.

For additional opera performances, see Index for following:

JAZZ- RAGTIME

DIXIELAND

CONCORD SUMMER JAZZ FESTIVAL
Concord, California

July for two consecutive weekends (six concerts)

Some of the veteran festival-goers recall with fond memories the first jazz concerts held in the grassy Concord Boulevard Park, where the facilities were makeshift, with a rented portable stage, and where there was usually a crisis. The difficulties ran the gamut: a poor sound system, sudden artist's cancellation, an extremely hot day when the sun baked the metal folding chairs making them impossible to sit upon, and an extremely cold day when the San Francisco Symphony had to wear topcoats and blankets while performing. Over these minor catastrophes, the festival prevailed, and things are different now. The informality still exists, but the festival has a new home.

The creation of Carl Jefferson, an energetic local Concord businessman, civic leader and avid jazz enthusiast, the festival was begun in 1969. Despite unprofessional facilities, Jefferson rounded up top-rank jazz professionals and produced concerts which gained civic support and the respect of large and loyal audiences. Nine years later, because of Jefferson's excellent track record and the backing of the city of Concord, the Mount Diablo Unified School District, and the community, the success of the festival paved the way for the construction of the Concord Pavilion, sometimes referred to as "The House That Jazz Built."

The festival has been described as low-keyed, middle-of-the-road jazz programming with a leaning towards the established and conventional jazz that hit its peak thirty years ago. Many jazz buffs feel that Concord's identity as a showcase for traditional jazz, and for the musicians who are not heard much anymore, is a point in its favor. For its tenth annual festival in 1978, many of the artists who had performed in early seasons were on hand to celebrate: Pearl Bailey, Louis Bellson, Paul Desmond, Ella Fitzgerald, Woody Herman, Benny Goodman, Earl "Fatha" Hines and his Quartet, Chuck Mangione, Herbie Mann, Peter Nero, Oscar Peterson Trio, George Shearing Quintet, Mel Torme, and Cal Tjader, to name a few of the many outstanding artists.

The Concord festival is located in the Mount Diablo foothills in Clayton Valley, thirty miles east of San Francisco. Concerts are held in the giant open-aired pavilion, an enormous geometric structure resembling something from outer space, which seats 3,555 people under an acre-square roof open on three sides. There is ample additional seating for 5,000 on the lawn.

Informality is the password at Concord, as the weather is usually balmy—twenty degrees warmer than San Francisco. The festival has been applauded on one hand and criticized on the other for not emphasizing the current and fashionable jazz enthusiasms, but as one jazz buff said, "It may be a mainstream, but it's a pretty good stream!"

For information and tickets write to: Concord Summer Jazz Festival Box Office, 2835 Willow Pass Rd., Concord, California 94522. Telephone: (415) 798-3311.

For accommodations write to: Concord Chamber of Commerce, 1331 Concord Avenue, Concord, California 94522. Telephone: (415) 685-1181.

MONTEREY JAZZ FESTIVAL
Monterey, California
Third weekend in September for three days

There is usually a great deal of applause, with cheers reverberating from the stands at the Monterey Fairgrounds during a rodeo, fair, or a horseshow, but none so enthusiastic and responsive as during the annual three-day Monterey Jazz Festival in September. Jimmy Lyons, a widely respected disc jockey on the West Coast is credited with starting the first festival in Monterey in 1958. During the first two decades, there were many memorable concerts—Dizzy Gillespie was frequently featured displaying his genius as the greatest of all contemporary trumpet players; one Sunday, six different symphonic brass ensembles performed a number of premiere compositions; Jimmy Witherspoon made his first appearance in 1959 and the Teagarden family—Jack, Charlie, Norma, and their mother were there in 1963. There were many world premieres at the festival—Jon Hendrick's *Evolution of the Blues Song,* Duke Ellington's *Suite Thursday,* Lalo Schifrin's *Gillespiana,* J.J. Johnson's *Perceptions,* Charles Mingus' *Meditations on Monterey,* and Gil Fuller's *On the Road to Monterey* are a few of the many performed. Much of the musical fare is devoted to jazz-as-before, but there are also many programs presenting new bands and new faces. Whatever the jazz style, Monterey has always enlisted talented jazz artists each year. Some of these well-known performers are Ruth Brown, Ron Carter, Benny Carter, Ornette Coleman, Red Garland, Dizzy Gillespie, Vince Guaraldi, Milt Jackson, Woody Herman, Carmen McRae, Thelonious

143

Monk, Gerry Mulligan, Odetta, Sonny Rollins, Pee Wee Russell, Bola Sete, and many, many more jazz greats.

The performances are held in an open arena at the Monterey Fairgrounds, one mile from the city of Monterey, located on the northern California coast, 120 miles south of San Francisco. There is seating for 7,000 fans, and a carnival-like atmosphere prevails during afternoon performances with booths lining the outside of the arena selling everything from sweet potato pies to tacos to beef teriyaki. The September weather on the Monterey Peninsula is usually ideal for the festival, with warm days and cool evenings. But there is always the possibility of the Monterey fog rolling in, so it is best to come prepared with a blanket or a warm coat!

The list of loyal fans and artists that keeps growing with every year, proves the theme of the Monterey Jazz Festival, "Keepin' the faith," is still working.

For information write to: Monterey Jazz Festival, P.O. Box Jazz, Monterey, California 93940. Telephone: (408) 373-3366.

For accommodations write to: Monterey Peninsula Chamber of Commerce, P.O. Box 1770, Monterey, California 93940. Telephone: (408) 649-3200.

SACRAMENTO DIXIELAND JUBILEE
Sacramento, California
Memorial Day weekend for three days

In the merry month of May, the Dixieland Jubilee is Sacramento's equivalent of May Day, Mardi Gras, *Fastelavn,* and *Oktoberfest,* all rolled into one. It's a festive three-day happening held annually over Memorial Day weekend. Bill Borcher, musician, educator, and Dixieland buff, started the first festival in 1974, along with some help from his friends in the Sacramento Traditional Jazz Society. Since the first year the Society has played host and sponsored the event. A few Dixieland jazz bands from various California jazz societies participated at the first festival, and as the word got around the following jubilees attracted Dixieland jazz performers from all over the country and the world.

The guest stars in the Dixieland jazz galaxy at the jubilees are numerous and bright: Billy Butterfield, Nick Fatool, Johnny Guarnieri, Bobby Hackett, Connie Haines, Peanuts Hucko, Ray Leatherwood, Abe Lincoln, Wingy Manone, Eddie Miller, Johnny

Mince, Abe Most, Jess Stacy, and Ted Wilson. Some of the bands from near and far were Pete Daily and the Chicagoans, Chicago; Turk Murphy Jazz Band, San Francisco; Rosie O'Grady's Good-time Jazz Band, Orlando; and Manny Treuman and his Bourbon Street Jazz Band, Tucson; and many more talented Dixieland jazz bands from the Sacramento area—the Gas House Gang, Sutterville Stompers, and the Capitol City Jazz Band, to name a few.

The evening concerts are appropriately staged by the levee in Old Sacramento at First and "I" Streets. The area once bustled with activity in the 1850s but crumbled into decay after 1900. In the spirit of preserving the old, Sacramento rebuilt the area in authentic style to capture the essence of the lively gold rush days!

The concerts are held in a huge open amphitheater with a graded pit so that the 4,500 fans are given a broad, picturesque view of the Sacramento River. The guest stars and bands, and talented local musicians, appear at the evening concerts. During the day, there are many smaller concerts at hotels, restaurants, and cabarets throughout the city. There are always continuous jam sessions going on, and often the jamming proves as lively as—or livelier than—the regular fare. So the jubilee claims, "If you thought that this kind of music you love is dead, don't worry. For three days at least, it will be alive and well in Sacramento. And thanks to jazz societies all over the world, it has been taken off the endangered species list and is recovering nicely!"

For information write to: Traditional Jazz Society, Box 15604, Sacramento, California 95815. Telephone: (916) 422-5277.

For accommodations write to: Sacramento Chamber of Commerce, 917 7th Street, P.O. Box 1017, Sacramento, California 95805. Telephone: (916) 443-3771.

BIX BEIDERBECKE MEMORIAL JAZZ FESTIVAL
Davenport, Iowa
Last weekend in July for three days

Bix Beiderbecke, the world-renowned and respected jazz cornet player, created musical history in his short life span of twenty-eight years. The Bix Beiderbecke Memorial Jazz Band, a group of East Coast musicians under the leadership of William Donahoe from New Jersey, met annually to honor Bix's memory. In a special tribute to the great jazzman on the fortieth

anniversary of his death in 1971, the band played at his graveside in his hometown of Davenport, Iowa. The reunion and the festivities which followed had such a strong emotional impact on the community that a Bix Beiderbecke Memorial Society was founded. Don O'Dette, president of the Society, was a moving force in the establishment of the Festival in 1972 with the goal of perpetuating the legend and memory of Bix and his music.

"Bix Lives," is the theme of the Memorial Jazz Festival which takes place for three days in late July. The Society renders a grand and glorious salute to Bix by inviting the very best jazz soloists and bands from all over the world to the festival. Musicians Bill Allred, Bill Challis, Hoagy Carmichael, Bill Krenz, Gene Krupa, Wingy Manone, Paul Mertz, Bill Mushlitz, Chauncey Morehouse, Bill Rank, Smokey Stover, Norma Teagarden, and Spiegel Wilcox are a few of the many greats who have appeared. The list of bands is equally impressive: Bob Barnard Jazz Band, Davenport Jazz Band, Fort Dodge Jazz Band, West Des Moines Dixieland Band, Memphis Nighthawks, Salty Dogs Band, Sons of Bix's, Smokey Stover Memorial Band, and W.C. Fields Memorial Jazz Band touch on the few out of the many who have perpetuated the spirit of Bix's music.

The musical styles and selections at the festival range from the earliest traditional jazz in the Bix manner to the full-blown concerts similar to the Jean Goldkette era. The devotees claim, "real Dixieland and the purest jazz fest anywhere!" Concerts are held on the banks of the Mississippi River in LeClaire Park. The musicians performing in a big bandshell have a dramatic and appropriate backdrop—the Mississippi River, with towboats and pleasure craft passing by. Spectators, often numbering in excess of 8,000 for a single concert, bring lawn chairs, blankets, and picnics, and sit under sunny skies or bright moonlight to enjoy the music. Nearby is a large circus-style tent which provides protection in case of rain, and shade for too much sunshine.

Though Bix Beiderbecke gained fame in his lifetime, he never forgot his hometown, and as shown by these musical tributes, Davenport has no intention of forgetting him!

For information and tickets write to: The Bix Beiderbecke Memorial Society, 2225 W. 17th Street, Davenport, Iowa 52804. Telephone: (319) 324-7170.

For accommodations write to: Chamber of Commerce, 404 Main Street, Davenport, Iowa 52801. Telephone: (319) 322-1706.

NEW ORLEANS JAZZ AND HERITAGE FESTIVAL
New Orleans, Louisiana
April for six days

New Orleans may rightfully boast of two major events each year: the Mardi Gras and the New Orleans Jazz and Heritage Festival. The forerunner of the festival was the New Orleans International Jazz Fest formed in 1968 to celebrate the city's 250th anniversary. Louis Armstrong, Duke Ellington, Peter

Fountain, and jazz bands from all over the world were on hand. When the Fest disbanded, jazz impresario George Wein, founder of the famed Newport Jazz Festival, urged the community to start a New Orleans festival to celebrate the regional culture of the city with music, local foods, and crafts. He felt it should be an open-aired event with people wandering about and enjoying the food, artisans, atmosphere, and of course, the music. That was the beginning of this great jazz festival in 1969.

The festival is divided into daytime and evening events held in various sites throughout the city; the Marriott Hotel, the Municipal Auditorium, the Royal Sonesta Hotel ballroom, Theatre of Performing Arts, and aboard the steamer *President* on the river.

The evening concerts feature a variety of New Orleans music—traditional and Dixieland jazz, ragtime, Cajun, country, rhythm, swing, blues, and gospel. The list of artists includes those who stand at the top of their class—Count Basie, McCoy Tyner, Allen Toussaint, Grover Washington Jr., Earl King, Dave Brubeck, B.B. King, Fats Domino, Ella Fitzgerald, Odetta, Muddy Waters, Roosevelt Sykes, Germaine Bazzle, as well as groups like Kit Thomas and his Preservation Jazz Band, the New York Jazz Band, the New York Jazz Repertory Company, Louis Cottrell's Heritage Hall Jazz Band, and the New Orleans Ragtime Orchestra.

One of the many memorable evenings of the 1978 season was a concert honoring ninety-five-year-old Eubie Blake, one of the pioneers of ragtime and jazz who helped put New Orleans on the musical map. He played several of his own tunes like, "I'm Just Wild About Harry" and "Memories of You." That same evening, Kid Thomas, another forerunner in the jazz and ragtime circles, played with his Preservation Hall Jazz Band, and the music went on and on and on.

During the daytime at the Louisiana Heritage Fair, held on the fairgrounds, there are stage shows continuously producing extravagantly different styles and kinds of music—Latin, folk, gospel, country, cajun, and contemporary jazz with musicians such as Al Belletto, Allen Fontenot and His Country Cajuns, Snookum Russell, Doc Watson, Sunnyland Slim and many more. The diversity of Louisiana culture is also shown in the food tents which serve indigenous foods—jambalaya, andouille, boudin, crawfish bisque, shrimp creole, muffalattes, stuffed crabs, chitlins, gumbo, frog legs, and roast beef "po-boys." In the craft tents local artisans display their wares.

For tickets write to: New Orleans Jazz and Heritage Foundation, Post Office Box 2530, New Orleans, Louisiana 70176. Telephone: (504) 522-4786.

For accommodations write to: New Orleans Chamber of Commerce, 301 Camp Street, New Orleans, Louisiana 70176. Telephone: (504) 524-1131.

ANNUAL NATIONAL RAGTIME FESTIVAL
Saint Louis, Missouri
Mid-June for six days

Ragtime lives in Saint Louis! On the levee, on the *Goldenrod* Showboat, each June, there is a joyous celebration in honor of ragtime. The birthplace of this American folk music was actually in the central Missouri city of Sedalia where Scott Joplin played his famous "Maple Leaf Rag" in 1899 at the Maple Leaf Club. Joplin moved to Saint Louis in 1903, and ragtime music skyrocketed to popularity all over the world! Ragtime continued to be popular until the beginning of World War I when the musical focus shifted to New Orleans and to traditional jazz. For over forty years ragtime was put to rest until the early 1960s when a group of young jazz purists, Trebor Jay Tichenor, Al Stricker, Bill Mason, Don Franz, and Frank Pierson, got together and formed the Saint Louis Ragtimers in hopes of preserving pure ragtime and traditional jazz. Pierson bought the old boat, *Goldenrod,* which had been lying dormant in the Saint Louis levee since 1937, and once again ragtime had a home—the first festival was formed in 1965 with the *Goldenrod* as the permanent festival site.

The festival features talented ragtime and traditional jazz performers and bands from all over the world. Turk Murphy and his band from San Francisco, legendery purveyor of ragtime and hard-core New Orleans jazz, the Salty Dogs from Chicago, Bix Beiderbecke Memorial Jazz Band, the Storyville Dandies from

Japan, Saint Louis Ragtimers, Mother's Boys, and Tiger Rag Forever Jazz Band, New Black Eagle Jazz Band, Ernie Carson Capitol City Jazz Band, and the David Reffkin's Ragtime String Ensemble are a few of the many dedicated bands who have performed in recent years. Some of the other talented artists have been Danny Barker, Eubie Blake, Ben Conroy, Jean Kittrell, Dave Jasen, Mike Montgomery, Butch Thompson, and Tex Wyndham.

During the six-day event, various decks, dining rooms, and lounges are used on the boat, as well as nearby barges. There's always room for a minimum of 1400 jazz and ragtime buffs. The music begins each evening at 6 P.M. and runs non-stop until 1 A.M. . . . and then there are always after-hours levee sessions which carry on until the early morning hours.

There is no doubt, the Annual National Ragtime Festival has become an institution in Saint Louis and a pilgrimage for people all over the world who love ragtime.

For information write to: Annual National Ragtime Festival, *Goldenrod* Showboat Landing, 400 North Wharf Street, St. Louis, Missouri 63102. Telephone: (314) 621-3311.

For accommodations write to: St. Louis Convention and Visitors Bureau, 500 North Broadway, St. Louis, Missouri 63102. Telephone: (314) 421-1023.

NEWPORT JAZZ FESTIVAL
New York City, New York
Late June to early July for ten days

The Newport Jazz Festival, the largest and most prestigious festival of its kind in the country, has as its hallmark the finest musicians in jazz—instrumental, vocal, big bands, and small combos—presented in novel and challenging situations. Founded in 1954 by Mr. and Mrs. Louis Lorillard and George Wein, jazz pianist and famed impresario, it was held for sixteen years in Newport, Rhode Island. Out-of-doors at Festival Field, the event attracted an average attendance of 50,000 jazz fans.

It was during the time at Newport when Mahalia Jackson dominated the gospel programs and when Miles Davis emerged as a potent force in the world of jazz. Then came the presentation of many rock groups that really did not belong at the jazz festival. In 1971, the festival was disrupted by a large number of

Elke

young people attending the concerts, and the era of the rural
Newport Jazz Festival was over. The following year, the festival
was brought to the biggest urban area in the country: New York
City.

Extending over ten days, the festival takes place in many
locations throughout the city: Carnegie Hall, Avery Fisher Hall,
Alice Tully Hall, New York University's Loeb Center, on a
Staten Island ferry, Roseland Ballroom, Washington Square
Park, and many other city street locations. It was recently
expanded to include a few events at Waterloo Village in

Stanhope, New Jersey, and at Saratoga Performing Arts Center in Saratoga Springs, New York.

The major part of the programming has been labeled by critics as mainstream jazz; the kind that makes you want to tap your feet. But the festival also offers a few programs featuring progressive, avant garde jazz. It rightfully boasts there is a style for everyone, for every age, and is held almost everywhere.

The Silver Jubilee in 1978 saluted the history of jazz. "Kid" Thomas, eighty-two, was there from Dixieland's past, and played with the Preservation Jazz Band; Count Basie, seventy-two, represented the swing era; Dizzy Gillespie emphasized the Latin beat; Betty Carter sang a tribute to the blues . . . and it went on and on with many other jazz greats from out of the glorious past.

Over the years the Newport Jazz Festival has attracted a long list of venerated stars, some of whom have been Laurindo Almeida, Count Basie, George Benson, Eubie Blake, Dave Brubeck, Charlie Byrd, Ornette Coleman, John Coltrane, Ella Fitzgerald, Stan Getz, Joao Gilberto, Lionel Hampton, Earl "Fatha" Hines, Herbie Hancock, Woody Herman, Stan Kenton, Charles Mingus, Gerry Mulligan, Buddy Rich, Sonny Rollins, Frank Sinatra, Mel Torme, and Sarah Vaughan.

For those who wonder what jazz is all about, *Webster's Dictionary* claims it is "a kind of music originally improvised but now also arranged, characterized by syncopation, rubato, heavily accented 4/4 time, dissonances, and unusual tonal effects . . ." Webster may be correct, but Louis Armstrong said it better; "If you have to ask what jazz is, you'll never know."

For information write to: Newport Jazz Festival, P.O. Box 1169, New York City, New York 10023. Telephone: (212) 787-2020.

For accommodations write to: New York Convention and Visitors' Bureau, Dept. J., 90 E. 42nd Street, New York City, New York 10017. Telephone: (212) 687-1300.

SUMMERGARDEN
New York City, New York
Early June to early September for fourteen weekends

One of the world's most inviting and famous "parks" is the open air Abby Aldrich Rockefeller Sculpture Garden in the Museum of Modern Art in midtown Manhattan. From early June to early September, the Garden is open to the public, without charge, every Friday, Saturday, and Sunday evening from 6 P.M. to 10 P.M. to enjoy the sculpture and the beautiful surroundings. On Friday and Saturday evenings, free informal concerts are presented as well. In 1971, the Mobil Oil Corporation made a grant to the city which enables the Museum to open its Garden Gate at 8 West 54th Street for these very special and well-attended Summergarden series. The Garden is an urban oasis complete with many famous sculptures, splashing fountains, reflecting pools, and beds of flowers, shrubs, and trees. The large-scale sculpture collection is an art exhibition in its own right, displaying works of such masters as Calder, Maillol, Matisse, Moore, Oldenburg, Renoir, and Rodin. Those in attendance at the series may sit, relax, stroll, listen to the music, and enjoy the surroundings in a setting fit for the Muses!

The emphasis at the concerts is on young emerging artists and composers who are provided support and exposure to new audiences. The programming, innovative, and always interesting, is usually organized into four month-long series with jazz, Dixieland, country, blues, and ragtime in June; classical and contemporary works in July; unusual "new music" in August; and a combination of all in September. Dance and movement performances are also included in the season, and in 1978, a series called "Projects: Performance" featured performance art.

Many young songwriters and composers have had their works performed and premiered at Summergarden. Some of the most recent have been John and Carrie Carney, Michael Cohen, John Guth, Garrett List, Joan La Barbara, Charles Morrow, Tom McLaughlin, Suni Paz, Carl Rosenstock, Marga Richter, Cecil Taylor, John Watts, and Peter Zumo. The list of soloists and ensembles is lengthy, and some of these talented performers are guitarist William Matthews; pianists Julie Holtzman, David Morgan, Dwight Peltzer, and Vivian Taylor; and ensembles Ecstasy, Artie Miller's No Gap Generation Jazz Band, Newband, Wall Street Dixieland Band, L'Arema Chamber Ensemble, Small Planet, and the Ambrosian Chamber Ensemble.

There have been many fascinating evenings at the Summergarden series. One such was in 1976 when Kirk Nurock's Natural Sound Workshop premiered a work entitled, *Track*, a musical composition on how movement effects sound. "Two men started singing and jogging towards each other, until they collided, chest to chest, causing the sound to change. Then a group of five, clustered together both physically and sonically, crossed the room slowly, shaking their heads vigorously to shake the sound." The same year, a series called, "Hit Tunes From Flop Shows" or "75 Years of the Great Music From Broadway's Biggest Turkeys" was presented. The audience (which usually averages 1,800 to 2,000, and had broken all attendance records to date) was told to guess the name of the show, and as a result, there was great interaction between audience and cast. The following year, concertgoers heard the premiere of two exciting works, both entitled *Wave Music,* by Charlie Morrow and Richard Hayman, which were played by forty unamplified celli.

Summergarden presents an exciting and interesting blend of the established masterworks in sculpture, along with the new, young, and sometimes experimental, presentations of music and dance!

For information write to: Summergarden, The Museum of Modern Art, 11 West 53rd Street, New York, New York 10019. Telephone: (212) 956-7298.

For accommodations write to: New York Convention and Visitors Bureau, 90 E. 42nd Street, New York City, New York 10017. Telephone: (212) 687-1300.

For additional jazz, ragtime, or Dixieland, see Index for following:

POPS

LIGHT CLASSICAL

STERN GROVE MIDSUMMER MUSIC FESTIVAL
San Francisco, California
Second week in June to the second week in August for ten Sundays

In typical San Francisco style, soloists at the Midsummer Music Festival at Stern Grove have ranged from Isaac Stern to the champion cable car bell ringer of the California Street Line, who performed with the San Francisco Symphony at Arthur Fiedler's request. "Sunday at the Grove," as it is called by San Franciscans, is a very popular tradition that has been going strong since the mid-1930s. The park, Stern Grove, was given as a gift to the city by music devotee, Mrs. Sigmund Stern, in memory of her husband who was a civic leader and philanthropist in San Francisco. Mrs. Stern had two objectives in mind: to present concerts which would give people an opportunity to hear fine music, and to provide employment for out-of-work musicians. Since the festival's first year in 1938, the San Francisco Park and Recreation Department has co-sponsored the event.

All concerts are free and held on ten consecutive Sunday afternoons. The programs consist of ballet, musical theater, dance troupes, instrumental soloists, orchestra performances, operas, jazz, and folk music. Artists and performing groups are not only from the San Francisco Bay area, but from all over the country. Well-known artists have performed at the Grove including Roy Bogas, Frankie Lane, Carlos Montoya, Jimmy Rogers, Pete Seeger, Isaac Stern, and David Del Tredici. Some of the groups have included the California Youth Symphony, Stan Kenton and his orchestra, Preservation Hall Jazz Band, Opera a la Carte of Los Angeles, Merola Opera (an affiliate of San Francisco Opera), Turk Murphy Band, Oakland Symphony, San Francisco Ballet, San Francisco Symphony, and Theatre Flamenco.

Stern Grove is a park adjacent to 19th and Sloat Boulevard in San Francisco. Covering thirty-five acres, it is famed for its natural beauty, and the trees have been planted to create a highly effective acoustical shell. Concertgoers usually come prepared for a full day of fun, relaxation, and the best in family entertainment, and bring sun umbrellas, cold beverages, picnics, as well as warm coats, blankets, and hot coffee. The "natives" already know, and out-of-town visitors should be aware of the possibility of a change in temperature, as the traditional San Francisco fog might creep in!

Average attendance at the Grove is between 15,000 to 19,000 patrons. At the 1978 season, the San Francisco Ballet drew its biggest attendance ever with approximately 22,000 ballet and music buffs filling not only the seating area, but the hills all around it! The special crowd-pleaser that day was "Q. a V." *(Quattro a Verdi)* "a showoff quasi-circus stunt piece" which had the crowds cheering with delight!

For information write to: Stern Grove Festival Association, P.O. Box 3250, San Francisco, California 94119. Telephone (415) 398-6551.

For accommodations write to: San Francisco Convention and Visitors Bureau, 1390 Market Street, San Francisco, California 94102. Telephone: (415) 626-5500.

GRANT PARK CONCERTS
Chicago, Illinois
Last week in June to the last week in August
for ten weeks

Thirty-five thousand people can't be all wrong—that's the normal attendance at the free performances during the summer festival in Grant Park in Chicago. Many of the audience have never seen the interior of a concert hall or an opera house, but have the experience and enjoyment of hearing first-class musical entertainment outdoors in the summertime. The City of Chicago began sponsoring free summer concerts in 1934 with adminstration provided by the Chicago Park District. For over forty years the concerts were held in Grant Park at the foot of Eleventh Street and Outer Drive, but in 1978 a new facility was built: the James C. Petrillo Music Shell, which is located at Columbus Drive and Jackson Boulevard. Now patrons have the added advantage of individual seating, unobstructed sight-lines of the stage, and superior acoustics, all within a lovely parklike setting.

The concert series extends over ten weeks with a minimum of forty-two concerts presented Wednesday through Saturday evenings. The Grant Park Symphony, the principal ensemble, is composed of musicians from the Lyric Opera of Chicago Orchestra, as well as other professional singers in the Chicago area. Symphonic works with vocalists and instrumentalists, opera in concert version, ballet, choral works, and pops are presented. Guest conductors and artists are invited to the series and have included Jorge Mester, Mitch Miller, Julius Rudel, Lee Schaenen, Leonard Slatkin, and David Zinman, conductors;

Malcolm Frager, David Golub, Mark Kaplan, and Ruth Slenczynska, instrumentalists; Martina Arroyo, Lili Crookasian, Sherrill Milnes, Beverly Sills, and William Warfield, vocalists. Thomas Peck is director of the Grant Park Symphony Chorus. During the 1978 season there was a memorable performance when the chorus presented Poulenc's *Gloria* and Rossini's *Stabat Mater* as a memorial concert to the beloved Thomas Schippers.

For information write to: Grant Park Concerts, Chicago Park District, 425 E. McFetridge Drive, Chicago, Illinois 60605. Telephone: (312) 294-2420.

For accommodations write to: Chicago Convention and Tourism Bureau, 332 S. Michigan, Chicago, Illinois 60604. Telephone: (312) 922-3530.

BOSTON POPS
Boston, Massachusetts
First week in May to the middle of July for nine or ten weeks

Merriment, camaraderie, and informality are the keywords which describe the atmosphere at the Boston Pops. Stately Symphony Hall is transformed into a musical drinking hall where concertgoers enjoy the light classics at their very best! When Henry Lee Higginson established the Boston Symphony Orchestra in 1881, he felt that Bostonians should have not only classical music, but also should be exposed to "less serious" music as well. Four years later, he founded the Music Hall Promenade Concerts and provided popular music, light classics, and refreshments to the patrons. "The Pops," as they soon began to be called, played at the Music Hall until the building was razed in 1899. The following year, the Pops moved into the new Symphony Hall where it has performed ever since. Considered to be acoustically one of the finest concert halls in the world, the auditorium seats 2,365 patrons—some seated at tables in the main part of the orchestra, and the remainder in the stalls around the auditorium.

In 1930, a young musician, Arthur Fiedler, who had started an outdoor musical series in Boston called the Esplanade Concerts, became conductor of the Boston Pops. Under his leadership, the Boston Pops has become an international musical institution.

Success has grown from Fiedler's brilliant programming, his idea of bringing back music of earlier days, and his sponsorship

of American music and young American soloists. The orchestra, composed of about ninety Boston Symphony Orchestra members, is conducted by Arthur Fiedler, as well as his assistant Harry Ellis Dickson. Performances are in the evenings Tuesdays through Sundays. Soloists engaged in recent years have been William Buckley, Tony Bennett, Ray Bolger, Julia Child, Glen Campbell, Ella Fitzgerald, Henry Mancini, and Mitch Miller.

The repertoire consists of light classics, current popular songs, medleys in arrangements, or movements from a symphonic work. Encores are the trademark of the Pops each evening — and though seemingly spontaneous, they are well-rehearsed and spirited presentations!

So, when in Boston, do as the Bostonians do, "Attend the Pops!"

For tickets write to: Boston Pops, Symphony Hall Box Office, Symphony Hall, Boston, Massachusetts 02115. Telephone: (617) 266-1492.

For accommodations write to: Boston Convention and Tourist Bureau, 900 Boylston Street, Boston, Massachusetts 02115. Telephone: (617) 536-4100.

ESPLANADE CONCERTS
Boston, Massachusetts
Mid-July for ten days

"Mr. Pops," the fabulous Arthur Fiedler, celebrated his golden anniversary with the Esplanade Concerts on July 4, 1978. Maestro Fiedler, the beloved musician and conductor, is a gentleman whose brilliant career has made an indelible mark on Boston's musical history and on the musical tastes of millions of people throughout the world. Born and raised in Boston, Fiedler and his family moved to Europe when he was around high school age and he studied music in Austria and Berlin. He returned to Boston in 1915 and joined the Boston Symphony Orchestra as a violinist. Fiedler spent several years promoting a series of free outdoor concerts, and these plans became a reality on July 4, 1929 when he conducted the first Esplanade Concerts in Boston under a hastily assembled wooden shell on the banks of the Charles River. The concert attracted an audience of 8,000.

Today, the concerts are held nightly over a two-week season in mid-July, a few days after the Boston Pops season has concluded. The musical offerings are pops, light classics, and excerpts from symphonic works. Like the Pops series, the Esplanade Concert Orchestra is composed of members of the Boston Symphony Orchestra and is conducted by Arthur Fiedler or his assistant, Harry Ellis Dickson.

The series is still given without charge and is a very popular musical event in Boston with normal attendance in excess of 20,000. The site remains the same, as the concerts are held outside in a large park with Storrow Drive on one side and the Charles River on the other, but the old shell has been replaced by the Hatch Memorial Shell, presented to the city as a gift in 1940. Many concertgoers bring picnic suppers, relax on the large grassy area, and enjoy the music in the informal beautiful setting; many others listen from the vantage point of boats anchored in the nearby Charles River lagoon.

One of the most popular concerts in the city's history was the spectacular Fourth of July Bicentennial celebration in 1976. In an overwhelming demonstration of a spirit of patriotism and goodwill, over 450,000 people attended the Esplanade concert to hear a unique and brilliant presentation of Tchaikovsky's 1812 Overture. The music was punctuated by the firing of cannons accompanied by amplified bell ringers, and nearby church bells were coordinated with a dramatic fireworks display. It was a memorable and fitting 200th-birthday celebration for Boston and for the nation!

For information write to: Esplanade Concerts, c/o Symphony Hall, Boston, Massachusetts 02115. Telephone: (617) 266-1492.

For accommodations write to: Boston Convention and Tourist Bureau, 900 Boylston Street, Boston, MA 02116. Telephone: (617) 536-4100.

SAINT LOUIS MUNICIPAL OPERA
Saint Louis, Missouri
*Last week in June to the first week in September
for ten weeks*

"Muny Opera," the name given the Saint Louis Municipal Opera, has stated that it is "America's oldest and best-known summer musical theatre." In the first season in 1919 just before the performance of *The Bohemian Girl,* a sudden rainstorm caused severe flooding of the nearby River des Peres. The waters of the river swelled to great heights running under the stage and ruining props, musical instruments, costumes, and scenery. The performers, staff, and community leaders united together to prepare makeshift scenery and costumes, and the following evening the show went on! With a beginning like that things could only get easier.

Muny Opera presently offers a wide range of the latest musical comedies, including traditional favorites and well-known popular performing groups, dance companies, and guest symphony orchestras and conductors. During the season eight or nine musicals are given five times a week along with four or five special events. There have been more than eighteen world stage premieres, among them, *Meet Me in Saint Louis, State Fair, Calamity Jane, Molly Darling,* and *Snow White and the Seven Dwarfs.* Muny Opera has brought to its stage talent from all areas of the entertainment world, and many comparative unknowns who, with the added prestige of performing with Muny, have gone on to international success. Among them are Red Skelton, Brian Sullivan, Agnes Moorhead, Virginia Mayo, Irene Dunne, Cary Grant, Jose Ferrer, Jean Madeira, and June Havoc.

The list of stars who have appeared over the years reads like a *Who's Who* of the performing arts: The Andrew Sisters, Pearl Bailey, Leonard Bernstein, Carol Burnett, Glen Campbell,

Margot Fonteyn, Bob Hope, Gene Kelly, John Denver, Zero Mostel, Cyril Ritchard, Giorgio Tozzi, and many more.

Forest Park, a 1400-acre site, adjacent to the west end of the residential section of Saint Louis is the location of the Muny Opera. The performances are staged in the Municipal Theatre, an open air amphitheatre with the world's largest outdoor stage, measuring 90 feet by 115 feet and seating 12,000. As the amphitheater has a gradual slope of 53 feet, patrons find an unobstructed view from any location in the audience. The group of men who founded Muny Opera specified that "a portion of the seating was to be set aside for those unable or disinclined to pay the admission price." Now 1,500 seats are available free of charge on a "first-come, first-serve" basis!

Write for tickets to: Box Office—St. Louis Muny Opera, Forest Park, St. Louis, Missouri 63112. Telephone: (314) 361-1900.

For accommodations write to: Convention and Visitors Bureau of Greater St. Louis, 500 North Broadway, St. Louis, Missouri 63102. Telephone: (314) 421-1023.

For additional pops and light classical performances, see Index for following:
Birmingham Festival of the Arts, Alabama
Hollywood Bowl Summer Series, California
San Francisco Symphony Summer Series, California
Central City Summer Festival, Colorado
Mississippi River Festival, Illinois
Ravinia Festival, Illinois
Pendleton Festival Symphony Summerfest, Indiana
Bar Harbor Music Festival, Maine
Tanglewood (Berkshire Music Festival), Massachusetts
Meadow Brook Music Festival, Michigan
National Music Camp, Michigan
White Mountains Festival of the Arts, New Hampshire
Waterloo Summer Music Festival, New Jersey
Chautauqua Summer Music Program, New York
Saratoga Performing Arts Center, New York
Brevard Music Center, North Carolina
Blossom Music Center, Ohio
Robin Hood Dell Concerts, Pennsylvania
Temple University Music Festival, Pennsylvania
Shenandoah Valley Music Festival, Virginia
Wolf Trap Farm, Virginia
Music Under the Stars, Wisconsin

FOLK-TRADITIONAL

OZARK FOLK FESTIVAL
Eureka Springs, Arkansas
Last week in October for four days

"Shunpiking" (a term used in Arkansas to describe traveling off the major highways and turnpikes) and attending the Ozark Folk Festival, head the list of interesting activities in Arkansas during October. And they both can be enjoyed when one attends the festival. Off the highways and 'pikes there are many scenic roads which traverse some of the most spectacular natural terrain in the South. About fifty miles north of Fayetteville on Route 62 is Eureka Springs, site of the Ozark Folk Festival and the oldest health spa and resort city in the Ozarks. Listed in the National Register of Historic Places, the community, with its narrow winding streets and picturesque houses and shops, much the same as they were during the 1880s, retains a great deal of the charm of that period. What better place for a folk festival?

The celebration, first held in 1948, was established for the purpose of preserving the folklore and music of the Ozarks. With this goal in mind, most of the events feature non-professional Ozark musicians playing mountain music on fiddles, banjos, guitars, jackass jawbones, harmonicas, dulcimers, and other non-electrified musical instruments. Only authentic and traditional Ozark music and songs are allowed — that means the music must be at least seventy years old, and of course, much of it dates back to Elizabethan times. Another attraction of the festivities are dancers: jig and clog, and square dance groups.

The Festival Queen Contest is held opening night, and during the day, activities include craft displays and public concerts in Basin Circle Park. There are always many spontaneous and impromptu performances and dances in the streets — a hallmark and tradition of the festival. In the evening all performances are held in the historic Municipal Auditorium which has seating for 1,200 folk music enthusiasts.

The Chamber of Commerce in Eureka Springs comments, "We shore hope you enjoy the annual Ozark Folk Festival," and we shore think you will!

For tickets and information write to: Ozark Folk Festival, c/o Chamber of Commerce, Post Office Box 551, Eureka Springs, Arkansas 72632. Telephone: (501) 253-8737.

For accommodations write to: Eureka Springs Chamber of Commerce,

P.O. Box 551, Eureka Springs, Arkansas 72632. Telephone: (501) 253-8737.

THE SAN DIEGO STATE UNIVERSITY FOLK AND OLD-TIME MUSIC FESTIVAL
San Diego, California
Late April for five days

"Recycling of tradition is one of the main themes of the festival," comments Lou Curtiss, member of the San Diego Friends of Old-Time Music, and founder of the San Diego Folk Festival in 1966. "What makes this festival so special is that it's about old-timers. The revivalists, the young performers, the cult heros, they are just so much frosting on the cake. They are often the ones you come to see, but we want you to see the veterans, the ones who paved the way for the traditional music that is played at the festival!"

Old-timers of the 1920s and 1930s are many of the ones who have been forgotten until they are rediscovered and appear at the festival. Being comparatively near Hollywood is an advantage since many of the old-timers retire, go into seclusion, or work without publicity in the Los Angeles area, and they welcome the opportunity to share their musical tradition with others. Great performers like Wilbur Ball and Cliff Carlisle, pioneer country recording artists, performed at the 1973 festival, and the occasion reunited two who had not played together for over fifty years! And there were Sam and Kirk McGee, old-timers who had played on the "Grand Ole Opry" radio broadcasts for over fifty years, who made their appearance at the 1975 festival, and so did Patsy Montana. Sam Chatmon, Mississippi Delta Blues songster of the early days has been a very special addition to most of the festivals. Other old-timers to appear at recent festivals have been bluesmen Tom Shaw, Robert Jeffery, and Robert Pete Williams; country artists Cousin Emmy, Hank Penny, the Hoosier Hot Shots, and Johnny Bond; and mountain performers Tommy Jarrell, Benny Thomasson, Roscoe Holcomb, Jean Ritchie, Nimrod Workman, and many, many more. Besides these fine performers, many various ethnic groups perform at the festival.

San Diego State University campus is the site of the festival. Concerts are held in the 1,000-seat Montezuma Hall in the Aztec Center, as well as in various rooms, theaters, and outdoor areas around the campus. During the festival, activities begin mid-morning and continue on into the evening when the featured concert is held. Special guests and performers offer workshops and mini-concerts during the day to share their expertise and experiences with others. Typical of some of these events are bawdy songs, dulcimer workshops, kids' folk songs for kids, Latin pop songs, logging songs, old-time fretless banjo, pagan imagery in English folk songs, rodeo songs, political parodies, Shaker music, songs of whales and whaling, street singing, and yodeling. The total of all these activities adds up to a festival which is very enjoyable, educational, nostalgic, and entertaining!

For information write to: Friends of Old-Time Music, c/o Lou Curtiss, 3611 Adams Street, San Diego, California 92116. Telephone: (714) 282-7833.

For accommodations write to: San Diego Chamber of Commerce, 233 A Street, Suite 300, San Diego, California 92101. Telephone: (714) 232-0124.

WESTERN REGIONAL FOLK FESTIVAL
Fort Barry/Cronkhite, California
Mid-October for three days

Filipino, Finnish, African, Japanese, Yiddish, Scottish, Mexican, Armenian, Chinese, American Indian, Hawaiian, and Irish, are among the ethnic groups represented at the Western Regional Folk Festival at Fort Barry in northern California. Since 1975, the musical event has been sponsored by the National Council for the Traditional Arts in cooperation with the Golden Gate National Recreation Area and is offered to the public without charge. The festival is a joyous three-day celebration of California's rich and varied musical heritage, and as it is an outgrowth of the community itself, it represents the acceptance of cultural diversity. And as is typical of many folk festivals, the musicians often gather in the evening after the scheduled concerts for "jamming." At the Western Regional, it's not unusual to see a mariachi player swapping chords and tunes with a member of an Irish folk group . . . it's all part of the exchange.

The festival concentrates on the performance of traditional, authentic music, and dancing is included in the performance if it's an integral part of the musical presentation. There are three stages set up during the day, offering informal recitals and workshops. A sampling of these are songs of social change, fiddle styles, exotic instruments as Uilleann pipes, kaval, and a hammered dulcimer, songs and dances of California north coast Indians, and gold rush songs.

The beautiful setting is another big plus in contributing to the festival's success and large attendance. The festival site is Fort Barry in the Golden Gate National Recreation area, a short distance across the Golden Gate Bridge in Marin County. A portable stage is set up at the end of a large grassy bowl, and festival-goers bring blankets, picnics, friends, and families and prepare for a full day of relaxation, fun and plenty of good music. The weather in October is usually balmy and clear, but visitors will be well-advised to take note of the area's fog warning and bring plenty of warm clothes . . . just in case.

For information write to: Western Regional Folk Festival, National Park Service, Golden Gate National Recreation Area, Fort Mason, San Francisco, California 94123. Telephone: (415) 556-0560.

For accommodations write to: San Francisco Convention and Visitors Bureau, 1390 Market Street, San Francisco. California 94102. Telephone: (415) 626-5500.

FESTIVAL OF AMERICAN FOLKLIFE
Washington, District of Columbia
Early October for five days

"The greatest family reunion in the country," best describes the Festival of American Folklife, for the festival talks about, sings about, and dramatizes America's unique cultural story. Started in 1967 by S. Dillon Ripley, secretary of the Smithsonian Institution, the festival is sponsored by the National Park Service and the Smithsonian, and has developed into the largest and most popular event in the nation's capital. Each year, the festival presents a special theme, and beginning in 1978 and for the four years following, the theme "community" has been chosen. The festival is described as "helping to maintain our system of cultural pluralism and the delights of diversity."

All activities at the American Folklife Festival are free and open daily from 10 A.M. to 5 P.M. The events are centered around the Washington Monument grounds at Fourteenth Street and Constitution Avenue in Washington. Many facilities are used

167

for the music, dancing, and demonstrations: the National Museum of Natural History, the National Museum of History and Technology, Renwick Gallery, and the Mall, for exhibits, workshops, and craft displays.

The 1978 festival offered many fascinating events — music from Appalachian coal fields, sleeping-car porter narrative workshop, butter-churning displays, children's games and songs, chants and cries of street hawkers and urban peddlers, tales of cab drivers, blues and gospel songs, Creole and Zydeco music from Texas-Louisiana oilfields, and many more. A very special feature was a workshop offered by a group of folklorists who interviewed festival-goers about their family customs. In turn, the participant is given suggestions for collecting his own family folklore and ideas for printing and mounting a family history.

And where in the world could a visitor learn in one day to make a fisherman's net, shuck oysters, carve a decoy, listen to music from Vera Cruz, Mexico, and watch a ceremonial dance of the San Juan Pueblo Indians? The answer: at the American Folklife Festival!

For information write to: American Folklife Festival, Smithsonian Institution, Washington, D.C. 20560. Telephone: (202) 381-5911.

For accommodations write to: Washington Area Convention and Visitors Association, 1129-20th Street, N.W., Washington, D.C. 20036. Telephone: (202) 857-5500.

FLORIDA FOLK FESTIVAL
White Springs, Florida
Last week in May for four days

Most of the year, there isn't much excitement in White Springs, Florida with its four gas stations, one general store, and a restaurant. But when May comes and its annual Florida Folk Festival arrives, the little community, situated on the shore of the Suwannee River, just north of Lake City in northern Florida, comes alive and bustles with activity. There is always a warm welcome for the country dancers, craftsmen, and fiddlers who arrive by the dozen. It's a true celebration of grass roots, for perhaps those who come hope to be reminded of earlier times, of the heritage of their state, and they come together for a short time to perpetuate the traditions of the pioneer days of Florida. The festival is music, dance, crafts, regional foods, storytelling, pine trees and sunshine. There are performances and workshops on animal and bird calls, water witching, clogging, concha shell playing, bone playing, whip cracking, tall tales, psaltery playing, dulcimers and whittlin', spirituals, musical sawyers, and just plain pickin' and singin'.

The first festival was held back in 1953 when Mrs. Ada Holding Miller, better known as "The Mother of Florida Folk Music," persuaded the Governor that "it would be a good thing for the community to host a folk festival." He took her advice; thousands have agreed with her, and in 1977 the festival celebrated its silver jubilee.

All activities take place in the lovely 250-acre Stephen Foster Center and begin each morning and continue through the evening. An amphitheater, situated within a glen ringed by moss-draped oak trees, offers 5,000 spectators shade by day and a glimpse of the stars at night.

"Cousin," Miss Thelma A. Boltin, has been festival director since 1954 and is an outstanding authority on folk music and the lore of Florida. She presides over each concert in the capacity of mistress of ceremonies. One can always count on her to be gowned in a bright, but authentic, calico dress with an enormous straw hat. Festival veterans recall in 1972, when the audience was predominantly young people, that "Cousin" Thelma told the shirtless and barefoot college boys, still wet from swimming in the Suwannee River, that they should go home and put on shirts before coming to listen to the concert. And they did!

The Florida Folk Festival is the kind of place where old friends meet, and where babes-in-arms and grandparents alike all have a good time.

For information write to: Florida Folk Festival, Stephen Foster Center, Post Office Box 265, White Springs, Florida 32096. Telephone: (904) 397-2192.

For accommodations write to: Lake City Chamber of Commerce, East Orange Street, Lake City, Florida 32055. Telephone: (904) 752-3690.

EISTEDDFOD FESTIVAL OF TRADITIONAL MUSIC AND CRAFTS
Southeastern Massachusetts University
North Dartmouth, Massachusetts
Last weekend in September for three days

Eisteddfod is a Welsh word meaning, "the coming together and sitting down of minstrels and bards." This is exactly what happens for three lively days in September, not in the country-side of Wales, but in southern Massachusetts in the small college community of North Dartmouth. Songsters, musicians, oldsters, and youngsters arrive on the scene with dulcimers, fiddles, concertinas, flutes, bagpipes, flageolets, clay ocarinas, jaw harps, and guitars, ready and eager to participate, listen, and enjoy the activities at this very special gathering. The musical preference is authentic traditional folk music with English, Irish, Scottish, and American origins, but recently many other ethnic groups have been represented. The repertoire presented is a rich variety of voices, instruments, types of songs, and regional styles.

Howard Glasser is the person credited with starting the *Eisteddfod* in 1971. A professional artist and teacher of drawing, graphic design, and calligraphy at Southeastern Massachusetts University, Glasser became interested in the music of Scotland, England, and Ireland when he traveled there in the 1960s. He began collecting music, and his hobby led him to introduce musical gatherings at Carnegie-Mellon University in 1961, which he called *"ceilidhs,"* a Scot-Gaelic word defined as "a gathering or partying of friends." The *ceilidhs* on the campus where he was a member of the faculty were so well-received by folk music devotees, amateurs, folklorists, and students that Glasser instigated three full days of traditional folk music and crafts called, *Eisteddfod.*

The success of *Eisteddfod* is attributed to the wide variety of serious performers, the lack of emphasis on big-name stars, and to the informal, personal, and non-competitive atmosphere which prevails. There are some well-known folk performers, who receive a modest fee to cover expenses, but there are an equal number of lesser-known musicians who are united in the common dedication of preserving traditional folk music and crafts. The performers actively participate in the *Eisteddfod;* they are accessible and are not separated or protected from the audience. After a musician performs he returns to the audience, gives a workshop, or perhaps joins a jam session. A sampling of the musicians who come from near and far—New England to Scotland—are Roy Bookbinder, Jerry Epstein, Norman Kennedy, Margaret MacArthur, Maggie Peirce, Bill Price, Royston Wood, and many others.

Besides the evening concerts and traditional craft displays, there are many free informal and formal workshops which are considered by most to be even more important than the evening concerts. The workshops vary from medieval literature, New England gravestones, and storytelling, to Northwind bluegrass, black jokers, blues and hardtimes, children's concerts, square dancing, and ragtime and old-timey.

The festival is held on the campus of Southeastern Massachusetts University in North Dartmouth, a small community in the southern region of the state. The concrete and stone buildings on campus produce a dramatic effect with cantilevered balconies, unusual walled angles, and bold open spaces. The evening concerts are held in the 800-seat auditorium and the daytime mini-concerts and workshops are held outside with unlimited space for attendees.

Eisteddfod is the kind of festival where unknowns often deliver the best music and where performers, craftsmen, and folk music enthusiasts can meet, enjoy, and learn from one another.

For information write to: Southeastern Massachusetts University *Eisteddfod,* Southeastern Massachusetts University, North Dartmouth, Massachusetts 02747. Telephone: (617) 678-7521.

For accommodations write to: New Bedford Chamber of Commerce, 227 Union Street, New Bedford, Massachusetts 02742. Telephone: (617) 999-5231.

NEW ENGLAND FOLK FESTIVAL
Natick, Massachusetts
Third weekend in April for three days

One of the distinguishing features of the New England Folk Festival is that it is the "friendly festival!" All singers, callers, musicians, dancers, craftspeople, exhibitors, organizers, and workers give their time and effort voluntarily; and everyone works together for the fun of creating one grand, glorious, and successful production each year in April. It is a participatory occasion since most people who attend join in the activites in some fashion or other, be it for dancing, jamming, sitting in, singing, or attending a workshop. Anyone playing an instrument is encouraged to bring it along and join some impromptu or scheduled jam session or workshop, and those who like to dance may join in with a group of their choice. As many people come in folk costumes, the brightly colored attire adds another dimension to the aura of unusual sights and sounds of the festival.

The first New England Folk Festival was held in Boston in 1944 and for twenty-five years it had twelve different locations throughout the New England area. It now has a permanent home in Natick, Massachusetts, a community twenty-four miles west of Boston, and enjoys the collaboration of the Natick

Recreation Department. The entrance fee is nominal and it is not unusual to have attendance in excess of 5,000 during the three-day event.

The festival has an unlimited variety of offerings: ethnic dance exhibitions, folk song sessions, instrumental jam sessions, roving musicians, square and contra dances traditional to New England, workshops, national food booths, and ethnic craft bazaars. Although the emphasis is on folk dancing, music in its many forms is an integral part of the festival, for as well as dancing, there is a festival dance orchestra composed of musicians from all over New England whose expertise and love of traditional music bring them together each year for this friendly occasion.

A few of the ethnic groups represented at the festival are Swedish, Lithuanian, English, Bulgarian, Finnish, Latvian, Portugese, Estonian, Scottish, and Israeli. The exhibits and craft bazaars range from colonial metalwork, Ukrainian decorated eggs, colored scrimshaw, to private collections of Spanish gypsy dresses, and fans from around the world.

The festival appeals to all ages, and children play an important part in the event. Saturday mornings are set aside for a children's jamboree so that the young can dance and play music for one another. Enthusiasm runs so high at the festival that many folk music devotees attending the events have returned to their own community and started their own local mini-folk festivals!

Natick High School is the site of the three-day celebration which begins on Friday evening and continues until Sunday evening. It could be compared to a six-ring circus, as there are many activities going on simultaneously—dancing for everyone in the Main Hall, jam sessions in the corridors and halls, national foods in the cafeteria, and many other events throughout the school. And if weather permits, programs are held outside around the school area.

At Natick High School, it's the halls, not the hills, which are alive with the sounds of music in April during the festival. It's a kaleidoscope of events which add up to a joyful and friendly musical experience for everyone who attends.

For information write to: New England Festival Association, 57 Roseland Street, Somerville, Massachusetts 02143. Telephone: (617) 354-2455.

For accommodations write to: Chamber of Commerce South Middlesex Area, 615 Concord Street, Framingham, Massachusetts 01701. Telephone: (617) 879-5600.

FOX HOLLOW FESTIVAL
OF TRADITIONAL MUSIC AND ARTS
Petersburg, New York

First weekend in August for three days

Fox Hollow has been labeled the "No-Star Music Festival," but more appropriately, it should be called the folk people's festival. The festival's claim to fame lies in the variety and caliber of its participants, many of whom are not national celebrities, but first-rate, highly respected practitioners of traditional folk art. For many it is one of the very few, carefully chosen appearances in their yearly concert schedule.

The festival was started in 1966 by Bob Beers and his wife, Evelyne. Bob Beers, a renowned folk musician, composer, and singer, had studied to be a concert violinist until a nerve disability caused him to give up his plans and he turned to music in the folk tradition. He had been deeply influenced by his grandfather, George Sullivan, an old-time fiddler and folklorist, described by Beers as a "kind of Library of Congress of folk songs." Beers got the idea for a festival site in 1965 when he was walking around his forty-acre homesite in Petersburg, New York (which is twenty miles east of Albany). He followed a family of foxes cavorting in the woods to a natural amphitheater and it was there that Beers decided to bring musicians for summer concerts. He named the site "Fox Hollow" and the following year, the festival began. The yearly musical gathering flourished under the inspiration, song, and guidance of the Beers family. When Bob Beers died in 1972 in a tragic auto accident, his wife carried on his musical tradition. Beer's widow, Evelyne, has described this unique festival as ". . . a musical one; it's for and about musicians and their songs and instruments. Its original conception as an informal three-day gathering for people in love with music has never really changed. But since good music tends to create beneficial spin-offs, there's so much else for people to enjoy: crafts, dancing, plays, good food." And that's exactly what has been happening at Fox Hollow.

One of the festival's traditions worthy of mention is its eclecticism . . . for not only are folk and bluegrass music played, but there is balalaika music, psaltry, Irish bodhrans, ethnic dancing, storytelling, puppet shows, bagpiping, bones instrumentation, lots of fiddling, and a great variety of workshops. To maintain the simplicity and warm, informal atmosphere, the attendance is limited to 3,500 people each day.

Fox Hollow is a very special musical event to those in the folk community. For those who have never attended and have a special feeling for authentic folk music, why not put Fox Hollow in your festival itinerary?

For information write to: Fox Hollow Festival, Petersburg, New York 12138. Telephone: (518) 658-3400.

For accommodations write to: Albany Chamber of Commerce, 9 State Street, Albany, New York 12200. Telephone: (518) 434-1214.

ASHEVILLE MOUNTAIN DANCE AND FOLK FESTIVAL
Asheville, North Carolina
The first Thursday, Friday, and Saturday in August

Bascom Lamar Lunsford, the Squire of South Turkey Creek in North Carolina, told all of his city friends he was worried that mountain music was dying out. He felt that the only way to save the music was to give the people back up in the coves a chance to be heard. On a warm summer evening in August, 1928, "Mr. Bascom" got some of his friends to help him rope off a section of Pack Square in downtown Asheville for a gathering he had planned for his mountain neighbors so they could dance and sing. They all came from such places as Hominy Valley, Laurel River, Spill Corn, Sandy Mush, Rabbit Ham, Soco Gap, and South Turkey Creek, naturally. That evening gathering was to become the oldest folk and dance festival in the country.

Each year since, dulcimer sweepers, tune bow and mouth harp players, mountain fiddlers, banjo pickers, and dancers come to Asheville to dance and play their music "along about sundown." The music sung and the dances danced are strongly reminiscent of the Scottish, English, and Irish ballads that had been kept pure in the coves and in the valleys between the Blue Ridge Mountains and the Great Smokies. They are the unwritten musical traditions and rituals handed down from generation to generation.

The festival emphasizes strict adherence to traditional music —dancing, singing, and playing the way it was done a long time ago. Competition is held for smooth dancing, clog dancing, old-time fiddler, and bluegrass fiddler.

The city park was the festival site until the mid-thirties when it moved to McCormick Field. The Second World War and rain made it necessary to move the festival inside to the 2400-seat Thomas Wolfe Auditorium in the Asheville Civic Center.

Nashville has its country music sound; Saint Louis, its ragtime; New Orleans, its jazz; but Asheville has southern Appalachian ancient music and is very proud of it.

For information write to: Asheville Mountain Dance and Folk Festival, Asheville Chamber of Commerce, P.O. Box 1011, Asheville, North Carolina 28802. Telephone: (704) 254-1981.

For accommodations write to: Asheville Chamber of Commerce, P.O. Box 1011, Asheville, North Carolina 28802. Telephone: (704) 254-1981.

PHILADELPHIA FOLK FESTIVAL
Philadelphia (Schwenksville), Pennsylvania
Last weekend in August for three days

The Philadelphia Folk Festival prefers being a low or no-voltage folk festival, for in the early 1970s it was dominated by contemporary pop groups and their electrified instruments. Now it has many more string instruments without amplification, and there is less intrusion on the true folk music sound.

The festival, sponsored by the Philadelphia Folksong Society, started in 1962 and was held in Paoli, west of Philadelphia. Pete Seeger was the inspiration behind the festival, and his influence, as well as that of his mentor, Woody Guthrie, continues to be felt at the festival.

The festivals are now held at Old Pool Farm, situated in the rolling wooded countryside northwest of Philadelphia near the community of Schwenksville. The main events are presented three consecutive evenings in an open-air stadium seating 10,000. During the daytime there are three areas near the stage which are used for various craft displays, workshops, and small concerts.

The artists and bands who have appeared at the festivals are talented and dedicated performers. Some of these are David Amram, Alistair Anderson, Roy Bookbinder, Michael Cooney, Woody Guthrie, Fred Holstein, Tom Paxton, Jean Ritchie, Jim Ringer, Pete Seeger, Suni Pazi, and U. Utah Phillips. The workshops have presented events with such provocative titles as "songs of the supernatural," "ecology in folk music," "old and New England dancing," "singing for nickels and dimes," "roads and rails," "music to work by," and many, many more.

The festival is gaining momentum and new audiences, thanks to the efforts of the Philadelphia Folksong Society; its members are singing their songs throughout the area. During the school year, it has presented folk music programs to the local schools and has met with great success. The young audiences have been most enthusiastic and clearly will become the folk performers and concertgoers of tomorrow.

For information write to: Philadelphia Folk Festival, 7113 Emlen Street, Philadelphia, Pennsylvania 19119. Telephone: (215) 247-1300.

For accommodations write to: Philadelphia Convention and Visitors Bureau, 1525 J.F. Kennedy Blvd., Philadelphia, Pennsylvania 19102. Telephone: (215) 864-1976.

NATIONAL FOLK FESTIVAL
Wolf Trap Farm, Vienna, Virginia
Late July or the beginning of August for three days

Since the 1930s, folk festivals have been a regular occurrence in various parts of the country. The one individual most responsible for the folk festival movement is Sarah Gertrude Knott, referred to as "the Fairy Godmother" of folk festivals. As a student at the University of North Carolina in 1920, Miss

Knott helped stage "folk dramas" and became intensely interested in the traditions of many immigrants from Europe whom she encountered in her recreation work. Her skills and involvement led her to put together her first folk festival in 1934. This was held in Saint Louis, Missouri, and involved 300 participants from 14 states. It was followed by festivals in Chattanooga, Tennessee; Chicago, Nashville, Oklahoma City, and Denver. Since 1971, the permanent home of the National Folk Festival has been Wolf Trap Farm.

The National Folk Festival which is sponsored by the National Council for the Traditional Arts, features traditional artists — that is, people who are presenting an art form such as crafts, music, dance, or storytelling that has been handed down to them through a number of generations, through their community, and through their families. Name artists are not emphasized; generally, performers are selected because they represent unique and interesting traditions. In recent years, some of these artists and groups have been Leonard Emanuel, International Hollerin' Champion; Lydia Mendoza, "The Lark of the Border"; Larry Older, "The Last of the Adirondack Minstrels"; The Tigua Indians, Pete Seeger, and the Oinkari Basque Dancers. Some of the many interesting workshops have been Fiddle Swapping, Historic Military Songs, Children's Songs and Stories, Country Music Heros, Arabic Dancers, Bullshooting and Stomach Steinway, Chinese Lion Dancers, and many more.

Performances are held on the grounds of Wolf Trap Farm, in the foothills of the Blue Ridge Mountains in Vienna, Virginia. It is an ideal setting for the festival, with its pastoral scenery and rolling hills, only sixteen miles from Washington, D.C. In the afternoon, four stages are set up on the grounds and demonstrations and workshops run simultaneously. In the evening, concerts are held in the Filene Center and feature about six or more groups. Seating is provided for 3,500 folk fans inside, under cover of the amphitheater's roof, and an additional 3,000 may be accommodated outside on the sloping lawn. For people interested in these unique art forms, or fascinated with the endless variety which Americana has to offer, the National Folk Festival promises fun, discovery, and good fellowship in a beautiful setting.

For information write to: National Folk Festival, c/o Wolf Trap Farm Park for the Performing Arts, 1624 Trap Road, Vienna, Virginia, 22180. Telephone: (703) 938-3800.

For accommodations write to: Washington Area Convention and Visitors Association, 1129 20th Street, N.W., Washington, D.C. 20036. Telephone: (202) 857-5500. Also Fairfax County Chamber of Commerce, 8550 Arlington Blvd., Fairfax, Virginia 22030. Telephone: (703) 560-4000.

NORTHWEST REGIONAL FOLKLIFE FESTIVAL
Seattle, Washington
Memorial Day weekend for four days

"A general grass-roots event with joyful representation from nearly every ethnic group in the Northwest," best describes the Northwest Regional Folklife Festival in Seattle. Started in 1972 with the concept of presenting the people of the northwest "doing what they do to entertain themselves and making things for their own use," the festival has grown to be the largest of its kind in the nation. All participants and festival workers contribute their time and talents on a voluntary basis and all events are open free to the public. Support has come from Seattleites, the Seattle Center, the Seattle Folklore Society, the National Park Service, FRAB Radio, and the National Council for Traditional Arts.

Although there are some professional musicians, the emphasis is almost entirely on amateur performers who must be residents of the states of Washington, Oregon, Idaho, and Alaska, or the province of British Columbia. This covers a lot of territory as demonstrated by the group of nineteen Eskimos from the village of Ohgsenakale in southwest Alaska, who took a week and a half to journey by bush plane, airline, ferry, and bus to the 1977 festival. Some of the fifty-five ethnic groups who have been participating in the festivals include Chinese, Irish, Black American, Greek, Rumanian, Croatian, Estonian, Ukrainian, Vietnamese, Thai, North Indian, Mexican, and Scandinavian.

Music and dance workshops, demonstrations of traditional and ethnic crafts and "open mikes" are an important feature of the festival, for they encourage participation by the festival visitor. Very often a spectator one year returns the next as a participant! Festival coordinator, Allan Swensson reported that the seventh annual festival in 1978 was better than ever with over 120,000 attending and over 1600 participants in the activities of music, dance, workshops, and crafts. A highlight of the seventh season was an Indian powwow sponsored by the

United Indians of All Tribes Foundation with over two dozen Indian tribes participating in dancing, singing, and drumming competitions for trophies and awards. Another special happening was a mime, drama and sign/sing-along given by the Canadian Theatre of the Deaf from Vancouver, B.C. and the Northwest Theatre of the Deaf from Vancouver, Washington.

The four-day festival is held in the Seattle Center, Memorial Day weekend, rain or shine where, during the daytime, a dozen different stages feature continuous music. In the evening, performances are held in the Seattle Center's 900-seat Playhouse and in the 3,000-seat Opera House.

The Folklife Festival breaks down the barrier between the performer and the audience by stressing participation. Everyone goes to the festival to have fun, share his traditional arts, and sample the diversity and exuberance of the music and dance. If one doesn't find his favorite kind of traditional music in Seattle, where else could he?

For information write to: Northwest Regional Folklife Festival, Seattle Center, 305 Harrison Street, Seattle, Washington 98109. Telephone: (206) 625-4409.

For accommodations write to: Seattle Convention and Visitors Bureau 1815 Seventh Ave., Seattle, Washington 98101. Telephone: (206) 447-7273.

BLUEGRASS

OLD-TIME FIDDLERS
COUNTRY

TENNESSEE VALLEY
OLD TIME FIDDLERS' CONVENTION
Athens, Alabama
First week in October for two days

In 1965, when a Nashville newspaper columnist bemoaned the apparent disappearance of old-time fiddling, presuming it had been replaced by the Nashville country music sound, fiddling devotee Bill Harrison, who was a member of a group in Limestone County, Alabama, decided to find others who still had an interest in fiddling, and helped organize two local fiddling contests. The reaction from the contests was so enthusiastic that Harrison, Mike Wallis, and Bill Holland, who had all been gathering at the home of seventy-year-old "Mr. Sam" McCracken, a revered old-time fiddler, for the purpose of fiddling and exchanging tunes and tales, started the Tennessee Old Time Fiddlers' Convention in 1967.

It was decided the convention would be held in the academic atmosphere of Athens College in hopes of dispelling the "tobacco road" image so long associated with old-time fiddling, but the real push behind the convention was the fiddling buffs who wanted to keep fiddlin' music alive!

Athens, Alabama, the small rural town where the two days of festivities are held is nestled in the Cumberland foothills midway between Nashville and Birmingham. There's a feeling of excitement in Athens as people gather for the convention for the joy of making and listening to old-time music. What makes the Tennessee Old Time Fiddlers' Convention special is authenticity. The tunes fiddled, picked, sung, and danced bear titles and content originating in early America. Some of these tunes had been lost to the flood of modern music and are being kept alive only by the young fiddling student enthusiasts and by the old-time fiddling men.

The usual proceedings for the two-day October celebration begin with Bill Harrison shooting off two anvils (which he calls a "pore man's cannon") . . . that's the official announcement that the convention is ready to begin. This is followed by concerts and competition in old-time singing, bluegrass banjo, bluegrass band, and jam sessions. The second day, Saturday, the fiddling contest begins at 10 A.M. and continues on into the night. Awards are given for the senior fiddler (sixty years and older), and the junior fiddler (fifty-nine years and younger) with the grand event a "fiddle off" between the senior and the junior winners to determine the Tennessee Valley Fiddle King. Some of the other contests and awards are for guitar, old-time banjo, dulcimer, mandolin, buck dancing, harmonica and more.

The contestants are judged on rhythm and timing, creativity, authenticity and taste, expression and execution. The rules are few, but are closely followed—no electric amplification or drums, two tunes for fiddlers in the eliminations and three tunes in the finals, and certain tunes such as "Orange Blossom Special" and "Listen to the Mockingbird" are prohibited because they tend to attract "trick fiddling" and they have been "played to death." The competition is held in Athens State College Gymnasium with a seating capacity for 4,000 spectators. Outside the gym there is room for several thousand more enthusiasts who are involved in listening, jamming, or dancing.

It takes a keen ear and lots of experience to determine fiddling style at the convention, but the old-time fiddlers know. The fiddling style predominating at Athens is "Southeastern" which is played faster than other styles and often with a short bow, called a "jiggy bow." Other fiddling styles heard are Northeastern, Northwestern, Canadian, and Texan. And real old-time devotees claim, "You can tell where a man is from by the way his fiddle talks."

For information write to: Bill Harrison, Route 4, Box 634, Madison, Alabama 35758. Telephone: (205) 837-4235.

For accommodations write to: Athens Chamber of Commerce, Post Office Box 150, Athens, Alabama 35611. Telephone: (205) 232-2600.

OLD TIME FIDDLER'S CONTEST AND FESTIVAL
Payson, Arizona
Last weekend in September for two days

In Payson, Arizona, happiness is going to the old-time fiddling contest in September. Everyone—contestants, judges, and the audience all seem to have a good time. It's the kind of music that's toe-tapping, spirited, and makes for dancing. The rules, though few, are enforced: "Dancing at specific times only, not during the contest portion of the festival."

The Federation of Old-time Fiddling Judges felt that a definition of this kind of music was required and came up with the following: "Music played on the fiddle or violin, which was developed in North America from the time of the early English settlements; that is composed of thousands of tunes of English,

Irish, Scottish, Scandinavian, Germanic, French, and native origin; that was and is still primarily passed on by tradition, very little being written down on paper; that is primarily dance music, not including any type of music that was not developed until after 1900."

The Payson Chamber of Commerce sponsored the first festival in 1970 and set up the event to be held in the center of town on the back of a flatbed truck with a few hundred spectators on hand. Soon thereafter it gained fame as contestants were attracted from all over the Southwest. The festival site was moved to the Payson Rodeo Grounds where there is now room for 300 old-time fiddler enthusiasts to sit under a covered grandstand and enjoy the contest, and plenty of room for an additional 3,000 people around the grandstand area.

The fiddling competition is determined by three judges, and the rules are generally that "all selections must be danceable folk tunes played in old-time fiddling fashion. The contestants are required to play a hoedown, waltz, and a tune of their choice." Awards are given for the best Arizona state old-time fiddler, senior champion (over sixty-five), junior fiddler (under seventeen), trick and fancy fiddling, and ladies' champion fiddler award. The Arizona fiddler who receives the highest score at the contest receives an award, a certificate entitling him to play at the National Fiddler's Contest in Weiser, and to the additional honor of having his picture hung in the National Fiddler's Hall of Fame in Weiser, Idaho. During the two-day event, a regular format is followed each year beginning with the national anthem, flag-raising ceremonies, a welcome by the mayor of Payson, pre-contest entertainment and activity — gospel singing or square dancing, followed by the contest, the awards, and then "singing, fiddling, and dancing on into the night."

Payson, situated at an elevation of 5,000 feet in Gila County, is in the center of Arizona, ninety miles north of Phoenix. It is beautiful country covered with tall pines and with many lakes and streams. To the north is the 7,000-foot Mogollon Rim, which towers 2,000 feet above Payson and runs for more than 100 miles across the state and into New Mexico. A visit to this region of Arizona during the fiddling contest gives a traveler an opportunity to enjoy old-time fiddling at its best and see some magnificent scenery.

For tickets and information write to: Old Time Fiddler's Contest, Payson Chamber of Commerce, Drawer A, Payson, Arizona 85541. Telephone: (602) 474-2994.

For accommodations write to: Payson Chamber of Commerce, Drawer A, Payson, Arizona 85541. Telephone: (602) 474-2994.

THE SAN DIEGO STATE UNIVERSITY FOLK AND OLD-TIME MUSIC FESTIVAL
San Diego, California
Late April for five days

"Recycling of tradition is one of the main themes of the festival," comments Lou Curtiss, member of the San Diego Friends of Old-Time Music, and founder of the San Diego Folk Festival in 1966. "What makes this festival so special is that it's about old-timers. The revivalists, the young performers, the cult heros, they are just so much frosting on the cake. They are often the ones you come to see, but we want you to see the veterans, the ones who paved the way for the traditional music that is played at the festival!"

Old-timers of the 1920s and 1930s are many of the ones who have been forgotten until they are rediscovered and appear at the festival. Being comparatively near Hollywood is an advantage since many of the old-timers retire, go into seclusion, or work without publicity in the Los Angeles area, and they welcome the opportunity to share their musical tradition with others. Great performers like Wilbur Ball and Cliff Carlisle, pioneer country recording artists, performed at the 1973 festival, and the occasion reunited two who had not played together for over fifty years! And there were Sam and Kirk McGee, old-timers who had played on the "Grand Ole Opry" radio-broadcasts for over fifty years, who made their appearance at the 1975 festival, and so did Patsy Montana. Sam Chatmon, Mississippi Delta Blues songster of the early days has been a very special addition to most of the festivals. Other old-timers to appear at recent festivals have been bluesmen Tom Shaw, Robert Jeffery, and Robert Pete Williams; country artists Cousin Emmy, Hank Penny, the Hoosier Hot Shots, and Johnny Bond; and mountain performers Tommy Jarrell, Benny Thomasson, Roscoe Holcomb, Jean Ritchie, Nimrod Workman, and many, many more. Besides these fine performers, many various ethnic groups perform at the festival.

San Diego State University campus is the site of the festival. Concerts are held in the 1,000-seat Montezuma Hall in the Aztec Center, as well as in various rooms, theaters, and outdoor areas around the campus. During the festival, activities begin mid-morning and continue on into the evening when the featured concert is held. Special guests and performers offer workshops and mini-concerts during the day to share their expertise and experiences with others. Typical of some of these events are bawdy songs, dulcimer workshops, kids' folk songs for kids, Latin pop songs, logging songs, old-time fretless banjo, pagan imagery in English folk songs, rodeo songs, political parodies, Shaker music, songs of whales and whaling, street singing, and yodeling. The total of all these activities adds up to a festival which is very enjoyable, educational, nostalgic, and entertaining!

For information write to: Friends of Old-Time Music, c/o Lou Curtiss, 3611 Adams Street, San Diego, California 92116. Telephone: (714) 282-7833.

For accommodations write to: San Diego Chamber of Commerce, 233 A Street, Suite 300, San Diego, California 92101. Telephone: (714) 232-0124.

NATIONAL OLDTIME FIDDLERS' CONTEST
Weiser, Idaho
Third week in June for one week

"He was a fiddler, and consequently a rogue." These words were written by Jonathan Swift at the beginning of the eighteenth century, and many Weiser residents would take Mr. Swift to task for this proclamation. Fiddling came to Weiser, Idaho in 1863 when a way station was established, and covered wagon immigrants stopped for rest and recreation, and entertained themselves with fiddling music. Weiser musicians maintained their keen interest in fiddling throughout the years, and in 1914, the first fiddling contest was initiated. Interest waned, however, and by 1940 the fiddling contests were reduced to mere intermission "fill-ins" during a dance festival. Fearing fiddle playing would become a lost art, Blaine Stubblefield, a member of the local Chamber of Commerce and long-time fiddling devotee, organized the first Northwest Mountain Fiddlers' Contest in 1953, with the purpose of preserving old-time fiddling. After the first festival, the purely local event attracted steadily increasing numbers of contestants and attendees and grew to national stature. In 1963, on the occasion of Idaho's Centennial, the festival officially became the National Oldtime Fiddlers' Contest.

The festival is now a major musical event in the United States and in 1978, for the twenty-fifth annual contest, over 285 fiddlers from all parts of the country registered for the big Silver Jubilee celebration. Awards are given to the champion fiddle performers in categories of national champion, national senior (over sixty-five), national ladies', national junior (under seventeen), best-liked fiddler, and top accompanist. Old-time fiddlers are pointing with pride to a new generation of grassroot players, the new emerging youngsters with a "good ear." These young people are encouraged to "try the fiddle," and an award for the junior-junior champion is now given for the best young fiddler under thirteen!

The contest has five judges who listen to the fiddler in a separate room where the music is piped in. The rules are few, but strictly observed: the contestant must play a waltz, hoedown, and a tune of his choice, not to exceed four minutes and with a maximum of two accompanists. Special judges also award prizes for the best fancy fiddling and for the fanciest-dressed man and woman fiddler. All fiddling events are held in the 2500-seat Weiser High School auditorium beginning at 8 A.M. and continuing until 11 P.M. and then there is always, "jamming, dancing, and whatever" at the Hospitality Center in downtown Weiser.

Not only does a trip to Weiser during the Oldtime Fiddlers' Contest in June offer a very special musical experience for a traveler, but it provides spectacular sightseeing and recreation opportunities. Weiser is the starting point for the Great Hells Canyon Seven Devils country. Hells Canyon, the deepest gorge on the North American continent, is north of Weiser and affords the finest recreation in the Northwest . . . swimming, fishing, hunting, boating, hiking, river rafting, and camping . . . and listening to old-time fiddling.

For information write to: National Oldtime Fiddlers' Contest, 10 East Idaho Street, Weiser, Idaho 83672. Telephone: (208) 549-0452.

For accommodations write to: Weiser Chamber of Commerce, 10 East Idaho Street, Weiser, Idaho 83672. Telephone: (208) 549-0452.

BEAN BLOSSOM BLUEGRASS FESTIVAL
Bean Blossom, Indiana
Spring for a period of five days

Bluegrass and Bill Monroe go together like waltzes and Strauss, swing and Gershwin, marches and Sousa. The origins of bluegrass are nearly four hundred years old; the musical style as it is known today originated with Bill Monroe, the father of bluegrass. A tenor and mandolin virtuoso, Monroe put together a band with four musicans in 1938, and in tribute to Bill's home state Kentucky, called themselves the Blue Grass Boys. In those early days, bluegrass might have conjured up the vision of ramshackle log cabins, abandoned iron or coal mines, and whiskey stills, but today bluegrass is far from that image. It is a very popular musical institution performed in major concert halls, college campuses, roadside taverns, nightclubs, and at festivals.

Musicologists have defined bluegrass as "polyphonic vocal and instrumental music played on certain unamplified instruments brought from the British Isles to Appalachian regions . . . a band typically consists of a five-string banjo and guitar, together with a fiddle, dobro guitar, mandolin, and bass fiddle." Also, bluegrass has been likened to chamber music in the intricate demands it makes upon the ensemble's precision, and has been likened to jazz in the quick reflexes it requires to respond to the spontaneous ideas from "hot licks" on the fiddle and the banjo. But no matter how bluegrass is defined, devotees, be they purists, or a variation thereof, are in agreement that at the festival everyone simply enjoys the pickin' and singin'.

The festival is held each spring at Bill Monroe's own 100-acre park in Bean Blossom, Indiana (that's 45 miles south of Indianapolis) and the land is suitable for pup tents, campers, and trailers which arrive on the scene by the dozens. The festival activities include musicians playing impromptu bluegrass, people attending workshops, and many thousands of fans who sit on plank benches listening to the competitions and concerts on the stage. A significant number of attendees are "parking lot pickers," which means amateurs who not only listen to bluegrass, but who play it. These people travel thousands of miles to attend the festival and, once there, are raring to find others with whom to make music—which they always do—and everyone "gets together and shindigs."

The best bluegrass performers appear at this festival, and some of the artists are Lester Flatt, the Country Gentlemen, the Clinch Mountain Boys, Jimmy Martin, James Monroe, Don Reno, Earl Scruggs, Jimmy Skinner, Osborne Brothers, the Stanley Brothers, Mac Wiseman and many, many others.

Bluegrass is solidly ingrained in the nation's musical fabric, and has won many fans all over the world. So, no matter where one lives or what his musical preference, everyone seems to enjoy bluegrass at Bean Blossom.

For information write: Monroe Bluegrass Festival Headquarters, 3819 Dickerson Road, Nashville, Tennessee 37207. Telephone: (615) 868-3333.

For accommodations write: Indianapolis Chamber of Commerce, 320 N. Meridan Street, Indianapolis, Indiana 46204. Telephone: (317) 635-4747.

OLD TIME FIDDLERS' CONVENTION
Union Grove, North Carolina
Easter weekend for three days

Between Harmony and Love Valley—and that's about fifty miles north of Charlotte, North Carolina—is Union Grove. Latest population census shows 125 residents, but each year during Easter week, more than 130,000 people swarm into Union Grove for the annual Old Time Fiddlers' Convention. The man who's running this show, J. Pierce Van Hoy claims, "It's the only show in town . . . it's the oldest and biggest festival in the South!" J. Pierce Van Hoy's father, H.P. Van Hoy, champion old-time fiddler and schoolmaster, organized the first convention back in 1924 to help pay off the mortgage on Union Grove High School. In the early days, the event was held for two days before Easter, and the school grounds were open to banjo pickers, mandolin and dulcimer players, clog dancers, and old-time fiddlers. The convention was held in the school gymnasium and auditorium for over forty-five years, but in 1971, because many of the young festival-goers became boisterous, over-enthusiastic, and out-of-control, the school grounds became "out-of-bounds" for the convention. J. Pierce Van Hoy moved the convention to his own homesite on seventy acres of rolling farmland where he welcomes campers, trailers, vans, and carloads of young fans and old-time fiddlers.

Some of the traditions established in the 1920s still remain—one-half of the gate receipts go to help support the school, and no brass instruments or drums are allowed. There still is competition for bluegrass, country, and old-time fiddlers who compete for cash prizes, ribbons, and trophies. And the festival always allows time to pay tribute to a special friend and a true old-timer. A rousing welcome was given at one of the conventions for De Witt "Snuffy" Jenkins, one of the last and very

189

best virtuosos on the musical washboard. "Snuffy" received a standing ovation for his rendition of his favorite tune which was accompanied by the Hired Hands of Columbia.

In 1977, Van Hoy built an amphitheater which accommodates a portion of the gate — 15,000 fans. Other visitors are "jamming" and often miss the scheduled shows and competition. So, if you are planning to go to Union Grove's Fiddlers' Convention, rest assured that you'll find plenty of old-time fiddlers, but they are beginning to feel that the huge crowds are taking away from the original spirit of the convention!

For information write to: Old Time Fiddlers' Convention, Box 38, Union Grove, North Carolina 28689. Telephone: (704) 539-4934.

For accommodations write to: Charlotte Chamber of Commerce, 129 W. Trade Street, P.O. Box 1867, Charlotte 28233. Telephone: (704) 377-6911.

OLE TIME FIDDLER'S AND BLUEGRASS FESTIVAL
Union Grove, North Carolina
Memorial Day for three days

"A wholesome atmosphere suitable for the whole family," and "Entrance by invitation only" are two of the distinctive features which make the Ole Time Fiddler's and Bluegrass Festival unique and sets it apart from the Fiddlers' Convention held in the same small community of Union Grove, North Carolina. The festival is a low-keyed family-oriented affair with a strong dedication to genuine old-time music. It isn't a formal event, but the only way a visitor can gain entrance is by a written invitation from coordinator Harper Van Hoy. He wants to limit the crowd to those most seriously interested in hearing the "purest mountain music this side of the Mississippi." The invitation is limited to 5,000 people who, by requesting and accepting the invitation, agree not to publicly display alcoholic beverages on the premises and not to bring their pets.

Harper A. Van Hoy organized the festival in 1970 for the purpose of preserving a tradition his father started in 1924 — the presentation of Southern Appalachian fiddler, folk, bluegrass music, and dance. There is competition in many categories: twin fiddlers, junior old-time and bluegrass bands, senior old-time and bluegrass bands and individual categories for instruments such as autoharp, banjo, fiddle, harmonica, mandolin, and many

others. To insure the preservation of old-time mountain music there is a very special certified old-time fiddler's category which requires that the competitor take an oath before competing that he has met these rather rigid rules: he must be over fifty-five years old; never have had any formal musical training; and have learned from other fiddlers older than himself. The contest brings about a spirit of camaraderie, respect, and fun among the old-timers as they swap yarns and tunes. The old-timers have their day in the sun, and the new bluegrass music-makers are also given their turn.

Workshops are an important part of the festival, and demonstrations and instruction are given for most of the instruments used in the competition, as well as in children's folk harmonies, story telling, and clogging. Guest artists display such talents as gospel singing, psaltry concerts, tall tale-telling, and many more.

The festival is held at Van Hoy's campground right in the middle of Union Grove, called Fiddler's Grove (that's fifty miles north of Charlotte). The site has a lake, woods, mowed fields, and a natural amphitheater with a stage and a cleared area for 5,000 spectators to bring their chairs and picnic lunches and to enjoy the activities.

Harper A. Van Hoy says, "It is a festival for those who genuinely appreciate folksy, friendly surroundings filled with lots of good old-time music, spirited competition, where old friendships are renewed and new friendships born." That's what Harper A. Van Hoy and Fiddler's Grove are all about!

For information write to: Harper A. Van Hoy, Ole Time Fiddler's and Bluegrass Festival, Fiddler's Grove, Inc., P.O. Box 11, Union Grove, North Carolina 28689. Telephone: (704) 539-4417.

For accommodations write to: Charlotte Chamber of Commerce, 129 W. Trade Street, P.O. Box 1867, Charlotte, North Carolina 28233. Telephone: (704) 377-6911.

INTERNATIONAL COUNTRY MUSIC FAN FAIR
Nashville, Tennessee
First week in June for six days

Nashville is synonymous with the Grand Ole Opry and is called, "Music City, U.S.A." For one week in early June, country music fan club members from all over the world convene at the International Country Music Fan Fair. It's almost certain that if you arrive without a club affiliation you'll go home *with* one.

The first Country Music Fan Fair was held in 1970, sponsored by the Country Music Association and the Grand Ole Opry, a lively musical institution which lays claim to having hosted the oldest continuing radio program in the United States—200 entertainers and over 63 acts!

During the six-day event the Fan Fair presents a large number of stage shows with famous singers, dancers, and musicians; a bluegrass concert; autograph and picture-taking sessions where fans can see and talk with the big-name country music stars; and hundreds of exhibits and booths with country music-related attractions. A sampling of these booths are the Marilyn Sellers Admiration and Cheering Society, the Navel Felts International

Fan Club, and the Merle Haggard Hospitality Booth. The climax of the week's fair on Sunday afternoon is reserved for the Grand Master's Fiddling Championships.

Some of the big-name stars at the festivals have been Bill Anderson and the Po Boys, Johnny Cash, Ralph Emery, Lester Flatt and the Nashville Grass, Merle Haggard, Jim and Jessie, Loretta Lynn, Bill Munroe and the Bluegrass Boys, Minnie Pearl, Dolly Parton, Ralph Stanley, Ernest Tubb, Conway Twitty, Mac Wiseman, and many, many more.

During the week, concerts are held in downtown Nashville at the Municipal Auditorium, and Sunday's event is held at "Opryland," ten miles northeast of Nashville. "Opryland," a 358-acre music-theme entertainment park, offers a visitor a variety of delights as many shows run continuously, featuring jazz, rock, country, and folk music.

The Country Music Fan Fair is billed as "The Closest Thing on Earth to Hillbilly Heaven." And perhaps it is.

For information write to: Fan Fair, Box 2138, Nashville, Tennessee 37214. Telephone: (615) 889-7503.

For accommodations write to: Chamber of Commerce, 161 4th Avenue North, Nashville, Tennessee 37219. Telephone: (615) 259-3900.

OLD FIDDLER'S CONVENTION
Galax, Virginia
Second weekend in August for three days

A first-timer at the Old Fiddler's Convention in Galax, Virginia who wants to see and hear it all shouldn't overlook an important center of activity—the parking lot. It is there that all of the musicians rehearse and try to get in tune, and where all the dancers and players try out their acts before they dare to go on the stage! With all the dancing, fiddling, and visiting in the lot, some of the bystanders think it's a better show than what's happening on stage.

Many hundreds of contestants come to the convention each year from all over the world to this small town, sixty miles southwest of Roanoke, not far from the North Carolina border. Many, many more come to see what's happening and be seen and to hear what's happening and be heard. The instruments at the convention range from mouth harps to enormous bull fiddles, and there is competition for cash prizes, trophies, and ribbons in the categories of guitar, mandolin, old-time and bluegrass fiddles, old-time and bluegrass bands, dulcimer, dobro, claw-hammer and bluegrass banjo, clog or flatfoot dancing, and folk singing. The rules state that only string instruments will be judged, no electrical instrument is allowed, only authentic folk songs will be used, and no taps are allowed in the dancing.

The Old Fiddler's Convention was originated in 1935 when a few members of Moose Lodge #733 needed a fund-raising event and started the contest. The convention was dedicated to "keeping alive the memories and sentiments of days gone by and making it possible for people of today to hear and enjoy the tunes of yesterday."

The first two years, the convention was held inside as contestants came from nearby counties of Grayson and Carroll, but by 1937, the number of participants and the spectators had increased so greatly that the convention was moved to Felts Park in Galax where it has remained ever since. Under a covered grandstand there is seating for 5,000 people, and outside there is a large area where thousands more may sit on blankets and enjoy the music from that vantage point. Enjoy they must, for at the 43rd convention in 1978 there were 1,328 contestants, and over 25,000 spectators during the three-day festivities.

There are two things the audience can always count on: no matter what distance a contestant travels to attend the convention (and they do come from near and far), when they get up to play, their tunes will be ones that have been handed down from generation to generation. . . . and everyone will have fun!

For information write to: Old Fiddler's Convention, Post Office Box 655, Galax, Virginia 24333 or to Oscar W. Hall, 328A Kenbrook Drive, Galax, Virginia 24333. Telephone: (703) 236-6355.

For accommodations: Galax Chamber of Commerce, 405 N. Main Street, Galax, Virginia 24333. Telephone: (703) 236-2184.

For additional performances of bluegrass, old-time fiddlers, or country music, see Index for following:

SUGGESTED READING LIST

Artis, Bob. *Bluegrass.* New York: Hawthorne, 1975.

Baggelaar, Kristin and Donald Milton. *Folk Music: More Than A Song.* New York: Thomas Y. Crowell, Co., 1976.

Bernstein, Martin and Martin Picker. *An Introduction to Music.* Englewood Cliffs: Prentice Hall, 1972.

Bookspan, Martin. *One Hundred One Masterpieces of Music & Their Composers.* New York: Doubleday & Co., 1968.

Cooper, Grosvenor. *Learning to Listen: A Handbook for Music.* Chicago: University of Chicago Press, 1957.

Cornfield, Robert. *Just Country.* New York: McGraw Hill, 1976.

Cross, Milton. *New Milton Cross' Complete Stories of Great Operas.* New York: Doubleday, 1955.

Einstein, Alfred. *Short History of Music.* New York: Vintage/Random, 1954.

Ewen, David. *The Complete Book of Classical Music.* Englewood Cliffs: Prentice Hall, 1965.

———. *Music for Millions: The Encyclopedia of Musical Masterpieces.* New York: Arco Publishing, 1944.

Feather, Leonard. *The Encyclopedia of Jazz.* New York: Horizon, 1960.

Gleason, Ralph. *Celebrating the Duke & Louis, Bessie, Billie, Bird, Carmen, Miles, Dizzy & Other Heroes.* Boston: Little, Brown & Co., 1975.

Hurst, Jack. *Grand Ole Opry.* New York: Harry N. Abrams, Inc., 1975.

Kerman, Joseph. *Opera as Drama.* New York: Vintage/Random, 1956.

Lawless, Ray. *Folksingers and Folk Songs in America.* New York: Duell, Sloan and Pearce, 1965.

Lomax, Alan. *Mr. Jelly Roll: The Fortunes of Jellyroll Morton, New Orleans Creole & Inventor.* Berkeley: University of California Press, 1973.

Malone, Bill C. *Country Music, U.S.A.: A Fifty Year History.* Austin: University of Texas Press, 1969.

Moore, Douglas. *A Guide to Musical Styles: From Madrigal to Modern Music.* New York: W.W. Norton & Co., 1963.

Morgenstern, Dan. *Jazz People.* New York: Harry N. Abrams, Inc., 1976.

Nettl, Bruno and Helen Myers. *Folk Music in the United States: An Introduction.* Detroit: Wayne State University Press, 1976.

Newman, Ernest. *Great Operas,* 2 vols. New York: Vintage/Random House, 1958.

Price, Steven P. *Old as the Hills: The Story of Bluegrass Music.* New York: Viking Press, 1975

Sandberg, Larry and Dick Weissman. *The Folk Music Sourcebook.* New York: Alfred A. Knopf, 1976.

Shapiro, Nat and Nat Hentoff, eds. *Hear Me Talkin' To Ya: The Story of Jazz By The Men Who Made It.* New York: Dover, 1966.

Siegmeister, Elie. *The New Music Lover's Handbook.* New York: Harvey House, Inc., 1973.

Stambler, Irwin and Grelun Landon. *Encyclopedia of Folk Country and Western Music.* New York: St. Martin's Press, 1969.

Stearns, Marshall W. *Story of Jazz.* New York: Oxford University Press, 1970.

SUGGESTED READING LIST FOR TRAVEL

Fodor, Eugene. *America.* New York: David MacKay, 1976.

Mobil Travel Guides. New York: Rand McNally and Company, 1976.

Discover Historic America. New York: Rand McNally and Company, 1976.

Simpson, Norman T. *Country Inns and Back Roads.* Stockbridge, Massachusetts: Berkshire Traveller Press, Inc., 1979.

Woodall's Campground Directory: North American Edition. Highland Park: Woodall Publishing Company, 1977.

SUGGESTED PERIODICALS

Bluegrass Unlimited, Box 111, Broad Run, Virginia 22014.

Country Music, KBO Publications, Inc., 475 Park Avenue South, New York, New York 10016.

Downbeat. Mahr Publications, Inc., 222 W. Adams Street, Chicago, Illinois 60606.

Hi Fidelity. Warren B. Syer, State Road, Great Barrington, Mass. 01230.

The Muleskinner. Central Missouri State College, Warrensburg, Missouri 64093.

Opera News. Metropolitan Opera Guild, 1865 Broadway, New York, New York 10023.

Pickin': The Magazine of Bluegrass and Old Time Country Music. 1 Saddle Road, Cedar Knolls, N.J. 07927.

Sing Out. 595 Broadway, New York City, New York 10012.

INDEX

Note: an asterisk indicates festivals which offer a summer music school in conjunction with the festival season.

Cover, Book Design by Jan Lindstrom
Illustrated by Celia Elke
Edited by Virginia Rowe
Printed in Dalton, Massachusetts, U.S.A. by Studley Press
The Berkshire Traveller Press, Stockbridge, Massachusetts 01262

1   2   3   4   5   6